People of Color: Casebook of Clinical Considerations

Gargi Roysircar and Allyssa Lanza

Acknowledgment

We thank Dr. Katherine Russell for guidance, feedback, and the book's cover.

Contents

Preface

There is a growing appreciation for applying cultural considerations to case conceptualization and treatment of mental health clients. However, theoretical shifts are often accompanied by a steep learning curve and a desire to simplify complex concepts. For instance, few counseling theories allow a reader to wrestle with real-life ambiguities, tensions, and fluidity that can come with intersectionality. Intersectionality is the experience of identifying with or belonging to two or more stigmatized groups when someone is a member of multiple disenfranchised groups that are statistically more likely to be negatively impacted and have fewer access to resources.

The goal of this book, *People of Color: Casebook of Clinical Considerations*, is to guide clinicians, researchers, teachers/trainers, and consultants in the psychology profession on how to think about lived experiences and challenges of people experiencing the push and pull of intersectional identities. While literature on social minority groups is limited, research on intersectional identities arising from membership in multiple marginalized societies is even more scarce. Ideally, mental health providers would be providing evidence-informed care for intersectional diversity; however, how can they when no sound methodology has been used with an intersectional population of interest, and whose structural invisibility might make it difficult to even identify and engage with them?

This book contains a different case vignette in each chapter with questions to stimulate thinking on client difficulties, as well as therapists' self-reflexivity on their personal reactions to the case. Each case presentation is followed with a literature review, theoretical understandings, and practice hypotheses in ways a provider might start working with a client by considering the areas of clinical practice, research, teaching and training, and consultation. Figures, tables, and a References list are included within each chapter. The selected vignettes were inspired by real cases and semi-biographical fiction/non-fiction narratives, and details have been changed to protect the identity of clients. The authors pose that their "complex" vignettes reflect the general population and are representative of clients they encounter in their work.

Each chapter highlights a different manifestation of ecological determinants of mental health, such as race, ethnicity, and indigenousness, sex, gender, sexual identity, class, religion, immigrant standing, employment, and education, as these statuses are located at intrapersonal, interpersonal, microsystemic, exosystemic, and macrosystemic levels. Societal systems and their contexts are interactive, and they affect at the individual level of personal and social identity and gender expression; at the microsystemic level with disparities in human resources; at the exosystemic level of unjust laws and acts for policing and healthcare; and at the macrosystemic level with norms of racism, colonization, ethnocentrism, internalized oppression/Whiteness, cisgenderism, power, and privilege. The authors present their critical consciousness about the oppressive status quo and encourage readers to be critical in their learning and social action on behalf of their clients.

Chapter 1 is a study of a young, immigrant woman student from India struggling with depression as she navigates living and working in the United States, as well as with her extended U.S. immigrant family. Theories reviewed include the ecological model, acculturation, the Western concept of depression, and the medical practice of diagnosis. Chapter 2 discusses the case of a Latinx veteran struggling with asexual identity issues amidst familial pressure to marry upon her return from war. Concepts reviewed include personal and social identity, gender identity, racial identity, women's empowerment, and asexual orientation. Chapter 3 covers the case of a bullied American Indian adolescent boy who is trying to obtain an education and build a social network. Topics reviewed include systemic disparities in social services, such as, reservation segregation, poor education, low employment, poverty, inadequate mental health and substance abuse treatment, lack of recognition of indigenous religious practices, historical trauma, and ableism.

Chapter 4 reviews the case of a widowed Pakistani Muslim woman living in the U.S. post-September 11, 2001, when her husband was killed in the terrorist attack. Concepts reviewed include transnationalism, extended family support, religious xenophobia in the United States, parenting as a single mother of a child with disabilities, heterosexual relations within one's cultural group and in the White American group, and internet and social networks. Chapter 5 explores the therapy of a Muslim college woman student seeking rape counseling from a White, woman therapist at a university mental health center. The Multicultural Relationship Competency model is introduced, reviewed, and applied to this client.

Appendix A includes activities designed to promote experiential learning of core concepts discussed in this book. Appendix B includes short case vignettes which can be used for continued trainee self-reflection and for classroom learning activities.

Suggested Uses of This Text

The book can be read as a unified text or as individual chapters. It was written primarily for those working in mental health, students preparing themselves for mental health professions, graduate courses in mental health such as multicultural counseling, practicum, supervision, and proseminars, and undergraduate multicultural psychology courses. Readers are encouraged to journal about their experience as they read the text, including noting their feelings, personal assumptions, and how they wish to apply the learned material to their life in a meaningful way.

Please consider using the following prompts to explore personal values, assumptions, biases, and opinions. When emotionally safe to do so, consider discussing the prompts in a group. Notice how your response may or may not change after reading each chapter.

Personal Reflection Prompts

- In reading a vignette first, what details stand out to me as "important"? Why do these points seem important to me?
- After reading the literature review, am I drawn to a specific conceptual model? Am I resistant to a suggested conceptualization? Why might that be?
- Does any vignette remind me of something personal? How has that shaped how I engage with the material?
- What additional research would help me better understand a case presentation?
- How do I apply the suggested literature into my work with clients who experience the tensions and fluidity of intersectional identities? Are the problems arising from intersectional identities summative? How do I generalize the research on "similar" populations to clients I serve?
- What types of intersectionality am I most drawn to? How does that strengthen my work? How does it inhibit my work? Is there something about myself and my community that might draw me to a particular intersectionality?
- What are my intersectional identities? How do these shape my work?

We also invite you to write a review of the *POC Casebook* or of a particular chapter. Thank you.

Gargi Roysircar and Allyssa Lanza

February, 2021

Chapter 1: Ecological Contexts: Case of an Immigrant Woman from India

As psychologists, we understand that our clients present to us not only as individuals, but as people in relation to others, communities, societies, cultures, and time. Based on Lewin's and Bronfenbrenner's environmental models, multiculturalism represents interactions between a person and their environment. We view ecological theory as a metatheory that is applicable to a range of populations, presenting issues, and therapies. Ecological theory provides a template that suggests what to include in our conceptualization of problems and how to focus our interventions, research, consultation, and training as a consequence. Understanding human behavior within ecological theory means we are looking at *systemic influences* and their *interactional nature*. The following case illustration and literature review seek to demonstrate how the multiple ecological systems shape clients lives. Subsequently, considerations for teaching, research, and consultation are explored.

Case Illustration—Maya

This case and its analysis are based on and modified from a publication by Roysircar, G., & Pignatiello, V. (2011). A multicultural-ecological tool: Conceptualization and practice with an Indian immigrant woman. Journal of Multicultural Counseling and Development, 39(3), 167-179; as well as by Roysircar G. (2013). Multicultural assessment: Individual and contextual dynamic sizing. In F. T. L. Leong & J. Trimble (Eds.), APA Handbook of multicultural psychology. Vol 1. Theory & Research (pp. 141-160). Washington, DC: APA.

Maya is a 28-year-old Asian Indian immigrant woman of Bengali heritage who has been referred to a university counseling center by one of her professors. Maya presented to the counseling center voluntarily. During her session, a psychiatrist diagnosed her with depression, prescribed anti-depression medication, and recommended Maya for therapy. In therapy, Maya has begun to share her history. She came to the United States (U.S.) four years prior and currently holds a green card. Her uncle, a well-established physician, was able to procure a work visa for her as a nurse's aide in a retirement home. The retirement home sponsored her green card status. Maya also works at Walmart as an accounting clerk and is attending graduate business school to get an MBA degree.

Maya came to the U.S. soon after her mother's death due to surgical complications. In India, Maya had lived all her life with her father and mother and her two older brothers in her parents' home in Kolkata. Maya's brothers, who are married, live with their families in this home, never having moved out. Maya's father and brothers work for the central and state governments and tend to spend their incomes on extravagances. This worries Maya because the family has financial problems.

Maya now lives in a college town in the Midwest with her maternal uncle, his wife, their two teenaged daughters, and their pre-teen son. Maya calls her uncle and aunt "father" and "mother." She calls her cousins "younger sisters" and "younger brother," who, in turn, call her "Didi," a respectful title for the "oldest sister." Maya's aunt and uncle have lived in the United States for 20 years and would describe themselves as upper middle class. They live in a wealthy, predominantly White neighborhood. Their children were born in the United States. Her uncle and aunt speak Bengali at home but break into English when thoughts do not have Bengali expressions. They eat traditional Bengali food. Their children speak Bengali-English jargon and like American cuisine. The family has adopted an American lifestyle to some degree.

Maya has brought much of the Bengali culture to her life in the United States. This includes her deceased mother's role of staying at home during her free time to take care of her adoptive siblings and the household. Maya's life in her new home is centered on preserving the life she knew in India. She cooks Bengali food and maintains the home diligently. Even though Maya can observe only a few Bengali traditions in her new home, she still feels a strong connection to her roots. Many of her traditions are deemed unacceptable by her cousins, though Maya cannot understand why.

Maya came to therapy because, in her words, "I feel confused about so many aspects of my life." She does not feel adequate in many areas of her life. These include her experiences of school, peers, home, living arrangements, a Bengali way of life, religious observances, being a woman, U.S. politics, employment policies, U.S. fashion, spoken American English, and casual social communication. Maya's entire way of life has changed. Although members of her adoptive family constantly surround her, as well as people at work and school, Maya feels alone. She feels isolated from her uncle, who is absorbed in his medical work. Maya says she misses her departed mother, but does not say that she misses her father, brothers, or their wives.

When asked whether she would return to India, she says, "No," that she had immigrated to live in the United States. Maya shared that in India, she would not get a high-paying job and would not be able to send her father money. She also reveals that she is not considered attractive enough (that is, not fair-skinned, petite) to have an arranged marriage, so she would not have a husband either—another area of her life in which she feels inadequate.

Personal Reflection Questions

- What feelings do you notice coming up as you read about Maya? How might these feelings support your understanding of Maya versus how might your feelings be an interpretation of how you imagine Maya herself feels?
- What immediate thoughts are coming to mind? Do you notice yourself asking questions that are based in trying to determine a diagnosis or treatment? What would it be like to focus on understanding Maya's story and experience?
- What are the various individuals, communities, organizational policies, nations, and belief systems that influence you? Are any of these already influencing the work you could do with Maya?

Discussion Questions Related to Maya

- What is it like for Maya to be an Asian Indian woman in the United Sates? What does she think her role is in her US adoptive family? What are her feelings about her two different occupational involvements? (individual system)
- Who are Maya's friends at the university and how close are they? Why did Maya leave India immediately after her mother's death? Do her "new" U.S. parents see her as a solution to housekeeping and childcare needs? How did her uncle and aunt in the United States come into the picture of her departure? What are the religious events in the local Indian community

that Maya attends? (microsystem)

- How do Maya's friends, peers, US family, and Indian community interact with each other? What was it like when Maya's uncle got her a job as a nurse's aide? What are the relationships between various systems (work, school, family, and the Indian community)? (mesosystem)

- How aware is Maya of her U.S. family's immigration diaspora? What is the work and neighborhood climate for Maya and her uncle and aunt? Are they accepted? Is the family aware of childcare and homecare services within the community? (exosystem)

- How does Maya view the Indian mores of being the eldest daughter--a privilege, a burden, or as culturally prescribed? How are sibling roles different in the United States? What is Maya's understanding of the culture of Midwest United States? Were her original and extended families enacting a cultural script for dealing with a family crisis "back home" in India? (macrosystem)

- Had Maya made plans to leave India prior to her mother's death, or did her mother's death change her status within her family? How would Maya describe her life before her mother's death? Did she feel herself to be a financial or social burden on her father and, if so, how did that change when she left India? Or, did some complicated family dynamic cause her departure? How did she experience this change? (chronosystem)

Literature Review

Ecological theory builds upon the work of Kurt Lewin (1936) who proposed that all human behavior must be understood as the outcome of a person's interaction with their environment. Bronfenbrenner (1995) further developed the person-environment theory by stating that behavior occurs within a set of contexts whose differentiation is represented by five systems, which are often graphically represented as concentric circles. Table 1 presents Bronfenbrenner's five systems with examples that illustrate each.

First, is the *microsystem*, which consists of local groups with which an individual, couple, or group is a member (e.g., family, neighborhood, school, work, peer groups, place of worship, and community resources, including healthcare services). Second, is the *mesosystem* that consists of interactions among the local groups within which an individual lives and shares membership: school, peers, family, work, place of worship, and social organizations. How these community units interact affects individual members (e.g., how the family interacts with one's school or how one's place of worship interacts with one's community). Third, is the *exosystem* that includes the context of policies, laws, and the government.

Fourth, is the macrosystem that encompasses all subordinate systems (i.e., exo, meso, micro, individual/personal). According to Bronfenbrenner (1979), the macrosystem represents broader cultural mores, sociopolitical norms, worldviews, and societal-level responses. These can effectively structure life implicitly or explicitly for members of society, including our clients and us as psychologists. The macrosystem structures societal experiences of privilege and oppression.

Table 1. *An Application of Bronfenbrenner's Ecological Systems*

System	Examples
Microsystem	Comprised of one's family, friends, neighbors, school/job, place of worship, organizations and cohorts (e.g., clubs or cultural groups).
Mesosystem	Comprised of the interaction between various microsystems (e.g., how one's family interacts with the school system). This system becomes increasingly complex as systems inevitably interact.
Exosystem	Comprised of the policies and procedures for various microsystem organizations as well as large, government-run organizations (e.g., Medicare, Medicaid, Social Security).
Macrosystem	Comprised of the federal government as well as a nation's values, beliefs, attitudes, methods of effecting change (e.g., through military, political, or financial practices).
Chronosystem	The influence of time on all subordinate systems (e.g., biological changes of aging). Another example is the change in national mores because of major events (e.g., a disaster or terrorist attack).

Note. Examples are not all-inclusive. They are based on Brofenbrenner's (1979) ecological model of development.

Fifth, is the *chronosystem*. The chronosystem was added by Bronfenbrenner (1995) after the original theory was developed. The chronosystem refers to life changes and transitions that affect people, localities, and society over time. Hence, these changes can reflect those that affect the microsystem (family deaths because of a disaster) or the macrosystem (immigration flow).

Acculturation Considerations

Before we make an ecological analysis of Maya's case at five systemic levels, we address the acculturation of immigrants and current research on this topic. Berry's (2001) model of acculturation shows that both immigrants and the receiving society are confronted with two major issues: (1) maintenance of cultural group characteristics/identity and (2) contact/relationship between the two groups. In this bidimensional model, individuals select different components of both cultures in a way where increasing identification with one culture does not entail decreasing identification with the other. Because heritage and mainstream cultural orientations are considered independently, research is comprehensive and empirically valid only when it uses a bidimensional measure of acculturation ("Americanization" and cultural identity retention) rather than a unidimensional measure that consists of a single continuum of high to low acculturation (Ryder et al., 2000; Roysircar et al., 2021).

Four major ways immigrants relate to the host culture have been identified: (a) *assimilation*—identifying only with the host culture and rejecting heritage identity; (b) *marginalization*—rejecting relationship with the host society and heritage identity; (c) *separation*—identifying only with heritage identity and rejecting relationship with the host society; and (d) *integration*—becoming bicultural by maintaining some traditions of the heritage culture while selectively taking on customs of the receiving culture. However, when the receiving society restricts the type of relations immigrants can have with mainstream society, like in the practice of segregation, all four adaptation modes may not be viable. For instance, integration is only possible when the host society is open to multiculturalism and internationalism, which are periodically affected by nationalistic attitudes and immigration policies of the United States.

Some scholars, however, have argued that the acculturation style of integration is psychologically the most adaptive (cf. Berry,1997; Farver et al., 2002; Inman et al., 2007; Kim, & Omizo, 2006; LaFromboise et al., 1993). In Western psychology, integration or accommodation is understood as a positive process and outcome, as in cognitive psychology and psychosocial identity development. Contrary to this position, research is evidencing the relationships of biculturalism of later generation immigrants/immigrant descended children and mental health issues of anxiety, depression, and the immigrant paradox (Han, 2011; Lau et al., 2013; Roysircar et al., 2021). A bicultural identity of an individual is uniquely challenged as it searches for compatibility between two different value systems.

As another example, many people describe themselves with a bicultural or multicultural identity (e.g., Chinese American, Vietnamese American, Korean American, Indian Caribbean American, Biracial Transgender Japanese), which may offer fluid intersectionality between multiple ethnic contexts. Research, thus, is needed on the bicultural identity that involves the salience of one particular aspect of identity over others, due to the influence of the specific context within which an individual presently interacts. Furthermore, members of one family can adopt different acculturation adaptations. In addition, particular nationality groups display distinct patterns of acculturation adaptations, depending upon whether they come from collectivistic or individualistic traditions.

Considerations for Clinical Practice

Markus and Kitayama (1998) stated that personality "is interdependent with the meanings and practices of particular sociocultural contexts. People develop their personalities over time through their active participation in the various social worlds in which they engage" (pp. 66-67). Maya is in the midst of a transnational transition from an Indian to a U.S. culture. In this way, she is not only managing a shift between one or two ecological systems, but rather is trying to balance 5 layers of internalized ecological systems which have been the basis of her identity, with an entirely new set of systems. She requests help in completing this transition culturally, emotionally, and socially, as well as physically. Maya does not suggest returning to her first culture as a possibility.

The sense of being "a mismatch" or "not fitting in" is universal and common among immigrant clients. It can evoke a feeling that something essential is missing, is present but toxic, or that a person simply does not fit into roles and relationships. In Maya's case, where many potential causes of distress are present, clinicians may try to discern just where Maya may experience herself or her interpersonal, cultural, and physical environment as a source of pain. Clinicians might consider what internal (dispositional) and external (social) resources lend Maya strengths, and what challenges complicate her life.

One strategy is to understand what it means for Maya to live in present contexts with a particular identity and history. From there, clinicians can identify sources of mismatch and possible solutions, drawing on Maya's personal and contextually derived strengths. Maya might be encouraged to explore how she might adapt to, change, or leave part of her environment for one that offers her more support. Whatever Maya chooses to do now, she can optimize her future person-environment interactions with her strengths and resilience.

A good place to start this clinical exploration process is Maya's ecological niche, the defined space where daily life occurs: specific individuals, physical environment (e.g., qualities of home or office space, climate), interpersonal environment (e.g., birth family in India, adoptive family in the United States, coworkers, friends, acquaintances in the neighborhood and in the Indian immigrant community), and customary activities (e.g., attending religious festivals, hobbies, recreation). The niche can provide a rich source of clues about the quality of the client's life. It can help clinicians see if a person's life is too small to allow them to grow or so large that the person feels overwhelmed and fragmented.

Ecologically minded clinicians will be especially concerned about Maya's experience of two life events: First, the death of her mother and her subsequent loss of her whole family of origin as she suddenly moves overseas; second, her "adoption" by her extended family that requires her to assimilate into the family quickly—as a daughter and a sibling with full status and responsibilities. Taken separately, clinicians see each family life transition signifying a new set of roles and responsibilities for Maya in the most intimate of her life contexts. This new set of roles and responsibilities reflects transitions within Maya's microsystem (ex. changes to family and support system), mesosystem (ex. changes to how Maya understands her interactions with school and employment), exosystem (ex. transitions to the healthcare system in the U.S.), macrosystem (ex. differences in societal views about women), and even chronosystem (ex. the impact of Maya's age as she manages these transitions' impacts, or larger shifts in American attitudes related to immigration during the coronavirus epidemic). For clinicians, it is essential to hold what it means for Maya to be untangling the immense complexity of all of these simultaneous shifts in the context of the death of a parent and the loss of her family.

Clinicians can begin to consider the role of contextual level factors and how they intersect with individual level factors in resilience. Much of the resilience research has focused on individual traits (or dispositions) that promote resilience (Bonanno, 2004; Seligman, 2011). Our view is that this puts the onus of resilience too much on the individual—a dynamic that might lead to blaming the individual if a challenge is not met with personal hardiness (Roysircar et al., 2017). It is important for us to consider external resources, sociocultural factors, religious affiliations, and affirming systems that support resilience (Roysircar et al., 2019a, b). Similarly, while trauma is considered a "global phenomenon" that characterizes the human condition, as psychologists we can work to understand the cultural context in which traumatic events unfold and are resolved with community engagement (Roysircar et al., 2017, 2019a, b).

Maya, for instance, reported mourning over the loss of her life in India. Clinicians, educators, consultants, and researchers should not assume that they can easily understand loss from a diagnosis of depression. Grief represents loss and disruption often complicated by internal, interpersonal, and systemic conflicts. The nature of Maya's relationship with her new family influences the mourning she is experiencing. How much of Maya's diagnosed depression is actually disenfranchised grief: grief that cannot be openly expressed and worked through because of a lack of recognition and support for doing so. Maya's grief and loss needs contextual sensitivity. A lack of awareness of cultural responses to loss can lead to misinterpretation of individual depressive reactions, failure to offer appropriate support and assistance that will be perceived as helpful, and may even offend the grieving person, creating a barrier to openness to psychologists.

In conjunction with the ecological model, clinical work with Maya would encourage a bidirectional relationship, meaning there is a give and take between both client and the provider of services. Issues of power and privilege will be addressed—moving the power dynamic away from the professional "expert" and locating it within the context of Maya's experience of herself and the professional relationship. We encourage psychologists to engage in cultural humility while understanding that clients are the experts of their lives. For instance, it is important for us to understand Maya's culturally based impressions about her symptoms. Doing so is thought to increase empathy and cultural humility (Gallardo, 2014). Similarly, researchers can investigate the dynamics of power and privilege in psychologists' work with clients, students, research participants, and consultees. Thus, researchers can inform our discipline about the dynamics of power and privilege experienced by our consumers. Through cultural humility and awareness of power and privilege, we can work with individuals, families, couples, groups, communities, and organizations in ways that respond to their experiences.

Considerations for Teaching and Training

Trainers and trainees can ponder the ecological model as it applies to Maya on multiple system levels. The interconnected nature of the systems lends to a discussion in which questions asked from one system level leads trainers and trainees to consider how Maya's interaction with other systems levels are influenced. For example, asking about Maya's relationship with her employer (mesosystem) may lead to consideration of differences between how she views her role as an employee when considering one nation's beliefs vs. another's (macrosystem), and in turn, whether or not she feels comfortable asking her employer to help her understand her benefits (exosystem).

Trainers and their trainees may discuss a variety of social support factors that complicate Maya's experiences of immigration. Maya has disconnected herself from a network of relationships in her first culture that have defined her very sense of self since birth. Educators and trainees ascertain whether the range and intensity of relationships in Maya's present interpersonal environment appear sufficient from her perspective to provide the recognition, safety, support, challenge, and caring that she needs to thrive in her relocation. Maya mentions no friends or social activities. Educators and trainees ask whether this pattern is normative for women of her status in her culture, or is it indicative of something about Maya's present life—for example, immigrant discrimination against her, her personal avoidance of contact, or her home responsibilities? How lonely is Maya, and why?

Turning attention to her new life, trainers and trainees wonder whether Maya had any previous relationships with her new family in the United States. Her immersion into the role of eldest daughter seems precipitous to Western educators and trainees but may or not be so for her. Did she have a similar family role in India, so that her responsibilities were familiar to her? Might Maya view these responsibilities as a privilege or a burden that was perhaps culturally prescribed (e.g., for an unmarried woman)? Was her extended family behaving magnanimously, beyond what typically occurs for a woman in her situation? Were both Maya and her family in India enacting a cultural script for dealing with a family crisis? Or did her new parents see her as a solution to housekeeping and childcare needs? These and similar questions help to establish how Maya views herself as a person within her present familial context.

Maya described a firm sense of connection to her Indian cultural value system. However, educators and trainees recognize that Maya's new family's comfort with her cultural identity cannot be taken for granted. There may be differences between Maya and her new family in religious practices and celebrations that complicate her acculturation. The degree to which her new family maintains their Indian cultural heritage may influence the degree to which Maya feels validated in holding onto her cultural identity.

Trainers and trainees may express that they understand little about the significance of Maya's relationship with her cousins/siblings. How are relationship tensions expressed? Did interpersonal communication norms permit an open resolution of issues with the knowledge and assistance of the parents? Did her cousins lose any privileges or special status upon her arrival? Did Maya know how to perform the "oldest daughter" role based on her life in India, or did she need to learn this role as her new family life progressed in the United States?

The broader community context is essential in understanding Maya's feelings of alienation. Trainers and trainees ask if there is an Asian Indian community where she lives that may give Maya more opportunity to simultaneously maintain her heritage cultural identity and gradually relate to the American aspects of her new life. If her new family's background is unique in her city or university, her cultural background is more likely to mark her as someone "different" in peers' eyes. A discussion of these possibilities answers questions about Maya's appropriate person-environment interactions. For example, educators and trainees consider Maya altering her interactions with others, changing her environment's climate (e.g., advocating for herself in the face of discrimination), or leaving the present environment for a more compatible one (e.g., finding a job within a culturally familiar context).

Questions posed by trainers about Maya's case on the chronosystem level include: What have been the changes in clothing, language use, and family composition and roles in her new life in the U.S.? The transition into different experiential states provides ethnographic researchers an understanding of not only the ever-changing nature of Maya's contexts (i.e., through immigration), but also how she experienced these changes at various ecological levels, and which changed with time. The changes are relevant to consultation on Maya as the changes approximate between two points in time, before and after her mother's death and her immigration to the United States.

As educators, psychologists must also consider how school and occupational roles contribute to Maya's distress. For example, Maya's general intelligence level, previous educational success, and facility with English as a second language will help identify school-related stresses. Determining whether she as a woman with an Indian heritage chose her major based on personal interests or because of family needs, expectations, or traditions will help clarify the level of satisfaction Maya is experiencing in her studies (Roysircar et al., 2010). The degree to which Maya's new space physically resembles her original home in terms of geographic topography, interpersonal density, and climate are important to consider: Does she find the space compatible with her needs and comfort levels? Do these comfort levels influence the level of engagement with various institutional structures?

Considerations for Research

Researchers doing an ethnographic interview with Maya may choose to pose queries such as: How do you view hierarchical seniority, accompanied with titles, in Indian families? How do you view the role of women in India vs. the United States? How do you view Indian women wearing saris? What is your experience of the Midwest United States culture? These questions can aid researchers in gleaning information about Maya's acculturation adaptation to the United States, connection to her life in India, and ability to navigate a new system of standards, expectations, and beliefs.

Regarding Maya, qualitative researchers determine that her presenting issue of acculturation to a second culture may be experienced by anyone undergoing a radical life change at a point in time, as well as it being specific to an Asian Indian immigrant woman. Research needs to consider the interaction of bidimensional acculturation with various factors: individual personality, different generations, class, sex, age, LGBTQ+ identities, immigrant discrimination, the model minority myth, values differences and communication difficulties between parents and children, help-seeking attitudes/utilization, stigma about mental health, and psychological problems. Thus, ecologically minded researchers look for within-group diversity among immigrants rather than assume sameness. Researchers give the example that a sequela of cross-national transitions can vary according to sex and culture of origin, and, therefore, Asian Indian women may face different issues than Latinx immigrant men. This research can be quantitative, qualitative, or mixed methods.

Considerations for Consultation

Maya has already been evaluated by her university's counseling services center as depressed and was prescribed medication. The fact that she followed through with this referral from a concerned professor suggests some comfort with a Western medical facility, but psychology consultants should not assume a trust in Western medicine.

Even though Maya has followed up on the referral, consultants can inform the student counseling center that she may not be comfortable with a Western approach to conceptualizing distress and may have her own culturally-based impressions concerning her symptoms, which would be important to understand. Consultants must also remember that how any client views medical diagnosis is crucial for their involvement with professional interventions. This goes back to understanding an individual's self-definition and the meanings connected to it (see Chapter 2 for self-definition). For Maya, depression, as understood by consultants, was imposed on her by diagnosis. Maya's demeanor may have always been quiet, modest, introverted, and serious. The process of being evaluated as depressed can be likened to having another racial or ethnic culture imposed on a culturally diverse person—a process that may generate feelings of confusion, nostalgia for normalcy, and hopelessness. Ecologically oriented consultants are aware of how psychiatric nosology might alter Maya's interactions at different ecological levels (personal, client-therapist relationship, native family, extended family, religious community, university, work, mental health clinic) rather than simply viewing mental health presentations as symptoms in and of themselves without a label.

Conclusion

The source of Maya's distress is most likely multifaceted. As a result, our work with Maya must take a multifaceted approach. An ecological approach is a viable model for clinical work, training, consultation, and research responding to Maya's experience. It provides a basis for understanding how various systems in Maya's current and past environments shape her life. Through psychotherapy and skills training, Maya can learn that small changes in one system (e.g., microsystem) can subsequently have an impact on other systems because of their fluid interactional nature.

References

Berry, J. W. (1997). Immigration, acculturation, and adaptation. *Applied Psychology, 46*(1), 5-34. https://doi.org/10.1111/j.1464-0597.1997.tb01087.x

Berry, J. W. (2001). A psychology of immigration. *Journal of Social Issues, 57*(3), 615-631. https://doi.org/10.1111/0022-4537.00231

Bonanno, G. A. (2004). Loss, trauma, and human resilience: Have we underestimated the human capacity to thrive after extremely aversive events? *American Psychologist, 59*(1), 20-28. https://doi.org/10.1037/0003-066x.59.1.20

Bronfenbrenner, U. (1979). *The ecology of human development: Experiments by nature and design.* Harvard University Press.

Bronfenbrenner, U. (n.d.). Developmental ecology through space and time: A future perspective. *Examining lives in context: Perspectives on the ecology of human development,* 619-647. https://doi.org/10.1037/10176-018

Bronfenbrenner, U., & Ceci, S. J. (1994). Nature-nurture reconceptualized in developmental perspective: A bioecological model. *Psychological Review, 101*(4), 568-586. https://doi.org/10.1037/0033-295x.101.4.568

Farver, J. A., Narang, S. K., & Bhadha, B. R. (2002). East meets west: Ethnic identity, acculturation, and conflict in Asian Indian families. *Journal of Family Psychology, 16*(3), 338-350. https://doi.org/10.1037/0893-3200.16.3.338

Gallardo, M. (2014). Developing cultural humility: Embracing race, privilege and power. https://doi.org/10.4135/9781483388076

Han, W. (2011). Bilingualism and academic achievement. *Child Development, 83*(1), 300-321. https://doi.org/10.1111/j.1467-8624.2011.01686.x

Inman, A. G., Howard, E. E., Beaumont, R. L., & Walker, J. A. (2007). Cultural transmission: Influence of contextual factors in Asian Indian immigrant parents' experiences. *Journal of Counseling Psychology, 54*(1), 93-100. https://doi.org/10.1037/0022-0167.54.1.93

Kim, B. S., & Omizo, M. M. (2006). Behavioral acculturation and enculturation and psychological functioning among Asian American College students. *Cultural Diversity and Ethnic Minority Psychology, 12*(2), 245-258. https://doi.org/10.1037/1099-9809.12.2.245

LaFromboise, T., Coleman, H. L., & Gerton, J. (1993). Psychological impact of biculturalism: Evidence and theory. *Psychological Bulletin, 114*(3), 395-412. https://doi.org/10.1037/0033-2909.114.3.395

Lau, A. S., Tsai, W., Shih, J., Liu, L. L., Hwang, W., & Takeuchi, D. T. (2013). The immigrant paradox among Asian American women: Are disparities in the burden of depression and anxiety paradoxical or explicable? *Journal of Consulting and Clinical Psychology, 81*(5), 901-911. https://doi.org/10.1037/a0032105

Lewin, K. (1936). Principles of topological psychology. https://doi.org/10.1037/10019-000

Markus, H. R., & Kitayama, S. (1998). The cultural psychology of personality. *Journal of Cross-Cultural Psychology, 29*(1), 63-87. https://doi.org/10.1177/0022022198291004

Roysircar, G., Carey, J., & Koroma, S. (2010). Asian Indian college students' science and math preferences: Influences of cultural contexts. *Journal of Career Development, 36*(4), 324-347. https://doi.org/10.1177/0894845309345671

Roysircar, G., Colvin, K. F., Afolayan, A. G., Thompson, A., & Robertson, T. W. (2017). Haitian children's resilience and vulnerability assessed with house–tree–person (HTP) drawings. *Traumatology, 23*(1), 68-81. https://doi.org/10.1037/trm0000090

Roysircar, G., Geisinger, K. F., & Thompson, A. (2019a). Haitian children's disaster trauma: Validation of pictorial assessment of resilience and vulnerability. *Journal of Black Psychology, 45*(4), 269-305. https://doi.org/10.1177/0095798419838126

Roysircar, G., Masseratagah, T., Tran, Q., Niezvestnaya, M., & Thompson, A. (2021, in press). Asian Indian immigrant youth anxiety: A model minority's generational differences Journal of Multicultural Counseling and Development.

Roysircar, G., Thompson, A., & Geisinger, K. F. (2019b). Trauma coping of mothers and children among poor people in Haiti: Mixed methods study of community-level research. *American Psychologist, 74*(9), 1189-1206. https://doi.org/10.1037/amp0000542

Ryder, A. G., Alden, L. E., & Paulhus, D. L. (2000). Is acculturation unidimensional or bidimensional? A head-to-head comparison in the prediction of personality, self-identity, and adjustment. *Journal of Personality and Social Psychology, 79*(1), 49-65. https://doi.org/10.1037/0022-3514.79.1.49

Seligman, M. E. (2011). *Flourish: A visionary new understanding of happiness and well-being.* Simon & Schuster.

Chapter 2: Self and Social Identities: The Case of a Latinx Veteran

While identity is something we hold as an individual, it is not formed independent from the environment. Thus, identity cannot exist as static, solitary, and removed from contextual influences. Rather, it is inherently flexible, multiplicitous, and influenced by contextual factors. Simply, identity is complex and fluid.

Ultimately, identity includes three, interrelated elements: the personal, the social, and the intersectional. On the intrapersonal level, identity comprises of unique personal qualities and experiences. This aspect of identity also acknowledges the impact of developmental factors on the individual. The interpersonal aspect of identity includes understanding oneself in context of interactions with others. This should be distinguished from identity within community and society, which includes a sense of self within a broader social network and within a larger sociopolitical context, respectively. Such a definition of identity seeks to accomplish two goals. First, it requires that identity be recognized for existing within multiple contexts. Second, this understanding of identity requires that we refrain from seeing these multiple contexts as independent, but instead recognize that they influence one another.

As psychologists, it is essential to consider the multiple identities of our clients. This not only includes how these identities may integrate, but also how they may come into conflict with each other, creating tension and difficulties within the self. For people of color in the United States (U.S.), the experience of competing and incongruent intrapersonal, interpersonal, and societal identities is common. The following case illustration and literature review seek to demonstrate the complex, interactional nature of identity and explore its clinical considerations.

Case Illustration—Linda

The authors thank Dr. Katherine Russell for her assistance with theoretical development of this chapter.

Linda is a 32-year-old, third generation Latinx, high-ranking medical officer in the U.S. Army, who has returned home from a tour in Syria. Linda started to have recurrent insomnia and nightmares the past several months. She has been noticeably despondent and lethargic and feels "lost and alone." She appears to be confused about who she is, given that she has returned to the U.S. without employment. Linda misses the excitement of the emergency room she worked in when stationed in Syria.

Linda is from a traditional Mexican American, Catholic, working-class family. Her ailing father, with whom she has always been very close, is dying from pancreatic cancer and not expected to live much longer. Her mother is distraught, but grateful that her daughter has returned home to help take care of her father in his final days, especially since there is little money for home care, and Linda's other siblings live out of state. Linda's father, who did not understand her decision to join the Army, seems obsessed with knowing she will find "the right man to take care of her" before he dies. He claims to be dreaming of attending her wedding before he "goes to heaven."

Linda described feeling more comfortable presenting a more socially stereotypic male character. She does not identify as lesbian, but she does not feel the term "heterosexual" describes her, either. She has many male friends, prefers "jeans and old flannels to pantsuits and heels," presents with a quiet, tough affect, and claims to "tell it like it is." She has had few relationships to speak of and wonders aloud if she would be "better off" (a position of privilege) as a lesbian, but she cannot seem to imagine herself sexually with another woman. In fact, she cannot imagine herself being sexual with anybody and wishes she experienced some sense of sexual attraction. Linda has sought therapy on the advice of her medical doctor at the Veterans Administration Hospital near her hometown. She is hoping to find her energy and to figure out who she is, now that she is back in the world she once understood so well.

Personal Reflection Questions

- What feelings do you notice coming up as you read about Linda? How might these feelings support your understanding of Linda versus how might your feelings be an interpretation of how you imagine Linda feels?
- What immediate thoughts are coming to mind? Do you notice yourself asking questions that are based in trying to determine a diagnosis or treatment? What would it be like to focus on understanding Linda's story and experience?
- How do define your own identity? What does this encompass? Have you considered who you are in terms of various systems?

Discussion Questions Related to Linda

- How does Linda identify?
- How do her different identities intersect to form the specific person Linda is?
- How do the different identities intertwine with Linda's presenting problem?
- What is important for Linda?
- What assumptions made by others have had an impact on Linda's life?
- As a clinician working with Linda, how would you develop rapport?
- How would you engage with Linda around the

> intrapersonal, interpersonal, community, and societal contexts of her identity?

Literature Review

Historically speaking, identity formation is an existential concept, which is presented as the search for a pre-existing authentic self to be discovered, with an individual being challenged to find a unique sense of self; identity formation is also conceptualized as ego identity, reflecting the psychoanalytic roots of Erikson's theory of developmental achievement (Moshman, 2007; Ginter et al., 2018). Thus, identity has been historically understood as the subjective experience of individuality, autonomy, and rationality. While individuality and autonomy are fundamental to personhood, a person is a rational agent that engages in reasoning, constructivism, and making choices (Moshman, 2007; Ginter et al., 2018). This conceptualization can be called personal identity.

However, individuals notice that they have several identities that are influenced by each of their multiple contexts, and, thus, they hold various understandings or self-definitions of themselves depending on the context they are located. This complexity of identity can thereby be seen as a relation of self to context, with an individual's ability to adapt their identity to context. Yet context itself is not always healthy. In certain situations, contextual influences may force individuals to adopt identities that conflict with their own self-defined identities to survive, a struggle that Linda is experiencing. The resulting struggle must not be conceptualized as solely within the individual, as an existential struggle, but a consequence of an individual making efforts to exist in an unhealthy system. Another example of an unhealthy systemic influence is ethnic gloss (Trimble & Dickson, 2005). Ethnic gloss either overgeneralizes individual experiences as applicable to all people in a social group or dichotomizes people (e.g., Muslims vs. Christians), essentially dividing aspects of self into fundamental groups. By doing so, the multiplicity of identity and the uniqueness of the combination of experiences this produces is not recognized. Thus, it becomes essential for us as psychologists to be aware of the multiple aspects of self.

As psychologists we can move beyond consideration of personal (Erikson, 1968) and social identities (Tajfel, 1982), and attend to how intersectionality (Cole, 2009) contributes to a diverse identity. Intersectionality includes attention to structural dynamics of how oppressions and privileges of race, ethnicity, class, sex, gender, sexuality, immigrant/refugee status, and religion may mediate and moderate client presentations, research data, and outcomes. As psychologists, we examine the axes of power (e.g., Latinx, a woman, questioning gender norms, questioning sexual orientation, working class, Catholic religion) within which a person is located, as these overlap and create intersections where all five axes meet to create an intersectional identity.

Self-Definition

An individual may identify with sociocultural terms, categories, and groups created by society-at-large. It is likely, however, that what may be true for many in a group may not be true for a specific individual. In addition, individuals may not necessarily connect with one part of their identity as much as another, and this might change depending upon contextual factors (e.g., the current group one is communicating with, age/development, setting). For example, Linda may have held her Mexican American identity differently when she was in Syria versus when she was living at home. As psychologists we engage in efforts to acknowledge this complexity of self-definition. In the case of Linda, it is important to not only understand what identities she may have, but also the nuanced ways in which Linda *connects* to each of these identities.

It is also essential to recognize that self-definition is created by the person themselves, instead of it being given to them by society (Jenkins, 1996). Adolescence has a specific focus on understanding identity, but it may also be a particular time when the youth is compelled to utilize societally prescribed definitions of self, causing adolescent conflicts and resolutions (Kuperminc et al., 2004). However, self-definition requires individuals be active in the process of identifying themselves. If individuals can experience self-definition as liberating and genuine, there is a possibility for an empowering experience. In this way, self-definition includes self-efficacy and self-worth (Kuperminc et al., 2004), and involves creating an overall positive sense of self.

Because privilege might vary between various groups one belongs to, with some groups having more visibility, support, and acceptance than others, this can influence how well someone can securely and safely explore all aspects of identity. In turn, the development of one's own self-definition may be affected by systemically created limitations/constraints (e.g., the glass ceiling, the bamboo ceiling). Thus, it is our responsibility, as mental health professionals, to foster a space that allows for the development of positive, unconstrained self-definition. This begins with our ability to review how clients see themselves and to explore how this understanding interplays with personal and societally prescribed identities.

Intersectional Identities

When an artist mixes yellow and blue, we do not call the resulting color yellow-blue. Instead, we see the product of this interaction as its own unique color of green. Similarly, multiple identities within an individual interact with one another, producing a unique identity experience. In this way, intersectionality is holistic rather than additive.

Intersectional identities meet at a nodal point, where overlapping layers of self-definition interact to ostensibly create a new identity entirely (Cho et al., 2013). Each of these layers interacts with the other in a different way, and the manner in which they overlap may vary with the context in which a person is located. Given the environment, culture, age, or temporal context of the individual, each component of identity confers different degrees of power that interact with each layer of society, from individual (intrapersonal), community (e.g., family members) to institutional (e.g., mental health access) to broader ecologies, like national politics. If each individual must negotiate between same and different points of identity, and the ways that these points interact change within different contexts, then it is natural that identity should shift and evolve between contexts and across time as well.

Oppressions of race, ethnicity, class, sex, gender, sexual orientation, and immigrant/refugee standing are different but often these are experienced simultaneously by a person in all social locations. For instance, in Linda's case, she is working class, Latinx, a woman, and a third-generation immigrant. She prefers a non-conforming gender presentation and an ambiguous sexual orientation. These reference group identities are experienced individually as well as at social group levels. However, these experiences are not a sum of discrete oppressions. Clarifying further, oppression is not experienced as an aggregate of Low-Class Privilege + Ethnicity + Gender + Sexual Orientation + Immigrant Status. Conceptualizing oppressions as arising from various social categorizations and looking for commonalities across these rather than looking at group-specific or single axial oppression differences are of interest to feminist intersectional researchers (Cole, 2009). Thus, intersectionality focuses on "the vexed dynamics of difference and the solidarity of sameness" (Cho et al., 2013, p. 787). Figure 1 illustrates the relationship of different elements of identity for many women.

Figure 1. *Example of Ecological Model of "Womanhood"*

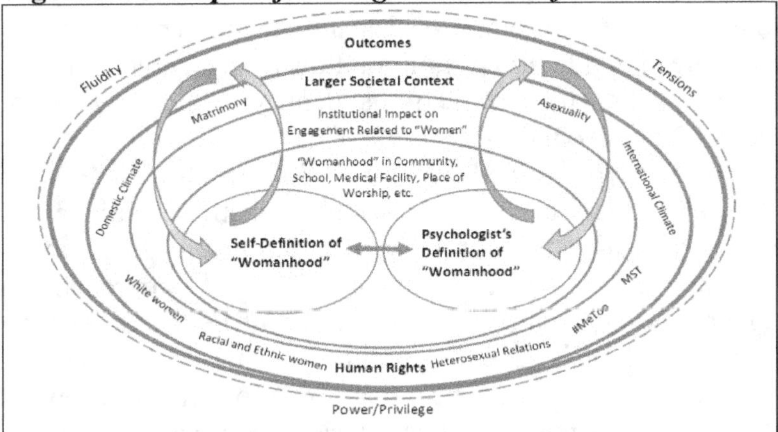

Note. This model has 5 layers of concentric circles that parallel the ecological systems. The levels bidirectionally interact within and between systems. They coalesce at level 5, *Outcomes*, which encompasses all prior levels. Surrounding level 5 are the additional layers that drive the ecological model: the dynamic processes of *power/privilege*, *tensions*, and *fluidity*. The authors thank Dr. Katherine Russell for her contribution of this figure. The figure is adapted from the APA Multicultural Guidelines (2017).

Linda's ethnicity, sex, class, traditional male interests, sexual orientation, and immigrant standing are not simply demographic status descriptors but encapsulate historical marginalization across the ecological macro, exo, micro, and individual systems and across the chronosystem. Thus, in our work as psychologists, it is important to view individuals as embedded in historical contexts and "take seriously the cultural and political history of groups, as well as the ways these socially constructed categories depend on one another for meaning and are jointly associated with outcomes" (Cole, 2009, p. 178). Specific components of identity may become more or less salient in a given context and may shift over time. Furthermore, one aspect of identity may be denied or suppressed to favor another aspect. For example, a male Latinx immigrant may not be able to access the parental nurturing side of his identity because of cultural expectations around masculinity.

A term coined in the 1980s in the context of antidiscrimination and social justice advocacy, intersectionality hones in on the limitations of "single axis" thinking in contrast to a multilayered approach to understanding identity so that we might better understand power and privilege (Grzanka, 2014). For example, individuals may experience discrimination directed toward them as a person who is Black/African American that might be different from the experience of discrimination as a woman, or discrimination directed specifically because they are a Black/African American woman (Cho et al., 2013).

The unique discrimination of Black women has been particularly relevant in the recent #MeToo movement, in which women of color, despite their key role in its origins, have felt alienated from it as White/White American women have become its representatives and have generated greater public interest. Thus, while women of color may identify as feminists as well as targets of sexual harassment, they may not feel a sense of belonging to the current #MeToo movement, which has not given proper attention to their heightened vulnerability to sexual harassment, nor to the decreased likelihood that harassment claims will be believed (Onwuachi-Willig, 2018).

Race, sex, gender, and class work dynamically to inform an individuated identity. Here oppressions and privileges, aspects of interlocking identities, are transformed by the intersections of multiple identities. Thus, as stated previously, intersectionality is more than the sum of its parts because it involves a transformation of inequalities (e.g., being gay) and privileges (being a White male) of unidimensional systems. Ratts (2017) defined intersectionality as "a tripartite relationship between identity, marginalization and privilege" (p. 91), noting that each component inherently carries status or a sense of whether that identity will lead to marginalization. As a result of intersecting identities, an individual can be both privileged and marginalized, or can be marginalized for multiple aspects of identity. Linear, unidimensional, discrete or "single axis" demographic variables assumed to cause between-group difference encourage the notion that all members of a structural category (e.g., third generation immigrant status like Linda's) have essentially the same experience.

In the case of Linda, there are several important intersectionality considerations. If examined with a simple, single-axis conceptualization, the first challenge would be deciding which contextual variable is the primary source of oppression or privilege from which to understand Linda's identity. Applying an ethnic minority framework, we may consider higher rates of depression among Latino/Latinas (Alegría et al., 2008) and the implications present for gender-role and/or sexual identity confusion. Similarly, psychologists could consider only the well-established power differentials relevant to working women, particularly those in male-dominated hierarchies such as the military. It is also tempting to consider the implications of Linda's traditional religious and conservative upbringing, and sudden role confusion as an adult woman living at home again, taking care of her parents after commanding the respect that comes from running a hospital on the frontlines of a battle-zone. As psychologists we could also examine Linda's experience of her working-class upbringing. These single analyses could be done in an additive manner, addressing separately each social identity. However, the self-definitional complexity of Linda's personal, social, and intersectional identities that make her a unique whole person would be disregarded.

Linda is not only a third-generation Mexican American woman and an intelligent successful American military leader from a working-class family, she is also confronting identity issues, potential war trauma, and mental health issues. It is not enough to consider single levels of disempowerment or potential empowerment. As psychologists we are encouraged to consider the interlocking of types and levels of disempowerment and their dynamic interactions within the contexts of privilege, history, group membership, and the female gender role of *marianismo* to be informed of Linda's confusions and struggles. Marianismo refers to Latina gender role phenomenon based on traditional cultural norms. We can strive to hold the multitude of structural contexts that inform Linda's experiences and identities to promote an understanding of underlying, implicit dynamics and, in so doing, work with her to facilitate a process of change.

Gender Identity

One example of intersectionality is understanding how womanhood might affect an individual within their culture or group. While there are many programs and organization focused on helping women, women who have two or more marginalized identities often do not benefit as significantly from the service. For example, White/White American women were the primary beneficiaries of the U.S. Affirmative Action program (Kendi, 2019), while women of color had relatively little benefit. In another example, Shalhoub-Kervorkian and Daher-Nashif (2013) speak about the global prevalence of violence against women. They note that this violence is often overlooked because it effects differently women of various intersectional identities. For example, violence towards young girls often looks different from violence toward senior women. Furthermore, the violence targeted toward senior women looks different in various cultures, as elders may be valued more or less in a particular culture. If a psychology professional were to assess for only one manifestation of violence, other types of gender violence could go overlooked. Often, it is only the concerns of the dominant group, e.g., corporate/institutional power of White American women are attended to, but the challenges of Black and Latinx women, who are underemployed while also serving as the primary caregivers of children and grandparents, are unrecognized and unaddressed (Ristock et al., 2017).

Gender and Asexuality

Gender, while traditionally considered a sex-based binary, is increasingly accepted as a socially created concept. While there are some biological differences, sex in and of itself is non-binary because it does not acknowledge people with chromosomal differences or who are intersex (Morgenroth & Ryan, 2020). Furthermore, there is documentation of nonbinary people in multiple cultures throughout history. Approximately 1 in 250 participants in a wide UK survey identified as gender nonbinary, and about 35% of cisgender U.S. men and women said that a part of them identifies with elements of the "other" gender. Gender identity and expression is important to consider, as some "…gender-minority individuals experience gender identity as reflecting a deep, innate, and immutable sense of self" (Morgenroth & Ryan, 2020, p. 5).

Morgenroth and Ryan (2020) consider a model of sex and gender expression. They speak about the performative nature of gender, which is well-engrained in individuals that it seems like an innate part of biological sex expression. The components of this performance include a character (often the gender assigned at birth), the costume (including gendered clothing and styling), a script (which guides expression of gendered interests and hobbies), the stage (physical and social environment where the performance is set), and the audience. When performances are not played "correctly," there can be social consequences. Those who create *gender trouble* challenge binary gender roles through elements of their gender performance (such as men wearing makeup and athletic women). Some groups, such as the LGBTQ+ community, are more open to varied gender performances; however, there are still more accepted roles, such as that of the *butch* or *femme* lesbian. Different types of *gender trouble* can lead to different challenges, including personal threats, group-based and identity threats, and systemic threats.

Historically, sexual orientation and gender expression were viewed as intertwined, such as the stereotype of the effeminate gay man (Cuthbert, 2019). Queer and feminist theories have explored the relationship between heteronormativity and patriarchy as symbiotic systems of oppression (Cuthbert, 2019). Other authors discuss how changing the cultural expectations linking intimacy and sex could have several relational benefits (Dawson, et al, 2016).

Asexuality represents a cluster of sexual orientations that include people who do not experience sexual attraction (Vares, 2018). While historically pathologized as resulting from both physical and psychological ailments (such as hormone disruptions and sexual developmental trauma), there is now a growing acceptance of asexuality as a valid identity (Dawson et al, 2016). Within asexuality are romantic and aromantic communities, including some who want a non-sexual intimate relationship. Also, within asexuality are demi-sexual and grey-sexual people who might develop sexual attraction under certain circumstances (most often once a meaningful relationship has developed). There are barriers asexual people face when trying to make romantic partnerships, especially when dating non-asexual people (Vares, 2018). Some asexual people may choose to have sex, sometimes to satisfy their partner and occasionally out of societal obligation. Additional barriers include feeling excluded. Despite barriers, asexual people have rewarding and healthy relationships, including friendships, physical affection (such as hugs and cuddling), and commitment.

Asexual people identify as gender nonconforming more often than other sexual orientations. In one survey, 26% of asexual respondents selected "none of the above" when given the options to identify as "woman/female" or "man/male" (Cuthbert, 2019). In a study of asexual, gender nonconforming people (Cuthbert, 2019), many respondents spoke about how gender was irrelevant to them. They described being aware of gender norms within society, but also not feeling the concept of gender was core to their individual identity. Some spoke about how they did not feel the need to define gender, as they were not interested in their physical sex organs. One participant spoke about wearing a sports bra, partially for comfort, and partially so their breasts would not be sexualized. Another participant spoke about how presenting more masculinely seemed to dissuade unwanted sexual attention.

Military Sexual Trauma and Gender Presentation

Linda's military experiences may have shaped her relationship with her gender expression and sexual orientation. Military Sexual Trauma (MST) affects approximately one in four women veterans (Brownstone et al., 2018). Women veterans tend to be sexualized early in their military experience, starting at recruitment and initial training. Many are told that there is an expectation that they will sexually engage with superiors to further their career.

An estimated 65%-79% of military women reported experiencing sexual harassment within the past year (Buchanan, et al., 2008). Even women officers, who often have more resources than their enlisted counterparts, are targets (Buchanan et al., 2008). Of military women who reported sexual assault, over half (52%) experienced social or occupational retaliation, including being assigned extra duties, threatened with discharge, and being reassigned to serve with their assailant (Dardis et al., 2018). Some women veterans commented that reporting of the sexual assault was worse and more traumatic than the assault itself (Brownstone et al., 2018). Many choose to not report and adopt the "code of silence" (Dardis et al., 2018).

Many women who have experienced MST have reported feelings of responsibility, which may stem from rape-myth acceptance (Dardis et al., 2018). Some feared they would be judged by others or not taken seriously. In interviews, some women blamed their feminine features, and believed that had they been less physically attractive, they may not have been targeted. For others, they found that clearly identifying as lesbian was a protective factor from being sexualized by others (Brownstone et al., 2018). Some women have tried to change their appearance, such as cutting their hair and binding their breasts, to try to protect themselves from future assaults (Brownstone et al., 2018).

Women who have experienced MST often have difficulties with relationships (Brownstone et al., 2018). Women survivors of MST reported their perpetrator was often someone they trusted, making it difficult for them to trust others in the future. Survivors may question their own judgement or feel they have lost the tough and physically powerful identity they gained in the military (Dardis et al., 2018). Furthermore, survivors are often betrayed by a judicial system that purports to support military employees but does not appropriately prosecute and punish perpetrators, increasing the mistrust of survivors. Sexual harassment occurs in many civilian workplaces, as well, with over one half of working women experiencing sexual harassment prior to retirement (Buchanan et al., 2008). Rates of harassment are higher for women of color (Buchanan et al., 2008).

Racial Identity

A discussion of identity is incomplete without referring to Janet Helms' (1995) Black racial identity development, which is about overcoming internalized racism, internalized societal racial stereotypes, and negative conceptions of the self and one's own group. The general development for a White racial identity is the abandonment of racism or entitlement. Healthy identity development for both Blacks and Whites is the capacity to be aware of and give up normative strategies of one's racial group for coping with racism. Sellers and colleagues (1998) explain that an individual's perception of what it means to be Black is the most valid indicator of racial identity; for instance, racial group membership may be an equally significant/important component of two individuals' self-concepts, but they may have very different meanings regarding what it means to be Black.

Cokley (2002) further developed the concept of internalized racialism, which occurs when one identifies with any stereotype attributed to one's racial group be it positive or negative, based on one's or others' false assumption that racial categories have immutable and innate characteristics. According to Hurtado, Alvarado, and Guillermo-Wann (2015), more than half of Black/African Americans (59%) think often or very often about their own racial social identity, even when in diverse settings, while more than half of White/White Americans (52.8%) never or seldom think about their racial identity. This disproportionate development of racial identity in Black

Americans and White Americans has negative implications for empathy within White therapist and Black client dyads (Helms & Cook, 1999).

Racializing Processes in Therapy

We enact racializing processes when we acknowledge racial difference in therapy and then deny the significance of the differences. In one study (Burkard & Knox, 2004), therapists who scored high on color-blindness reported significantly less empathy than did those who scored in the low range for color-blind racial attitudes. Enacting racial dynamics is a reality of racial dyads. Yet the therapeutic relationship can still be a place where an individual can feel understood and contained despite the negative influence of larger social forces (i.e., systemic racism). Generating new meanings minimizes the influence of negative societal pressures. A failure to create new meanings can arise when therapists and clients, who differ in race, unconsciously or consciously enact stereotyped interchanges, preventing the development of a truly allied therapeutic space.

Considerations for Clinical Practice

Identity competent therapy incorporates racial and ethnic identities, but also salient identities regarding sexual orientation, class, religion, disability, and/or gender, among others. In this way, a client becomes more than their cultural heritage, but rather a dynamic being with shifting emphasis on salient components of identity in each context. As such, every therapeutic encounter is a negotiation of sameness and difference, and every client is a diverse client.

Furthermore, the attitudes and ideologies of culture are constantly interacting with and influencing identities. Through a focus on how macro-level contexts of oppression and stereotypes inform community and personal biases, we can work with our clients to develop a formulation for their surrounding localities as they relate to their identities and biases. As psychologists we can also recognize how our own range of identities interact with those of our clients, engaging our differences as well as commonalities that have an impact on our work together. This intersectional framework encourages a depth of curiosity that translates into the change process, both personal and social (Cho et al., 2013). Using the intersectional framework, we as psychologists can work with our clients on how identity formation arouses cultural awareness and facilitates identity expressions, all leading towards the change process.

To explore intersectionality with Linda, for example, the method of "ask the other question" may be used. For instance, when we see something that is sexist in Linda's experience with her father and mother, we can ask ourselves, "Where is the heterosexism in this? Where is the Latina gender role in this?" When we see something that is homophobic, we can ask, "Where is the cultural issue in this? Where is the religious issue in this?" When we see the devaluation of a successful woman, we can ask, "Where is the patriarchy in this? Where is the class issue in this?" Intersectionality practitioners also ask themselves questions to practice self-reflexivity, so that they can critique their own work and refine their ideas and practices (Clough & Fine, 2007; Roysircar, 2004, 2009). Thus, intersectionality provides psychologists both a paradigmatic shift from personal and social identities to intersectional identities, as well as a psychotherapeutic change framework.

It is also important that, as psychologists, we begin to understand ourselves from an intersectional perspective. This means that we parse our own tangled webs of identification and our respective privileges or disadvantages. Moreover, in the clinician role, we can analyze these points of view in relation to individual clients to determine which parts of their identities might be consonant or dissonant in relation to their experiences and our experiences. Doing so will enable us to better understand our countertransference.

When we as psychologists, along with our clients, are open about our intersecting identities, the process gives voice to various interactions of power and privilege that each individual holds in the therapeutic relationship. It is hoped that this acknowledgement of intersectionality lends to an egalitarian therapeutic relationship. We encourage psychologists to acknowledge when one of a client's identities is an area where we lack knowledge. The client is then placed in an expert role with regard to that aspect of their identity, although this perceived client expertise is encouraged when we as the psychologist also bring an understanding of intersecting identities. The feminist model encourages us as psychologists to engage in self-disclosure of intersecting identities to explore individual and other identities of the client and ourselves. According to Dee Watts-Jones (2010), there may be vulnerability for the therapist in sharing a subjugated identity (such as being a Mormon) that is not overt to a client, especially when the client is privileged in that identity, such as in mainstream religion or spirituality (Catholicism in Linda's case).

The Gender Unicorn can be a useful visual tool to help discuss gender identity, gender, expression, sex assigned at birth, physical attraction, and emotional attraction (https://transstudent.org/gender/). The layout normalizes that each domain is independent of another, that each element exists on a spectrum, and that someone might change their responses at different times. It is particularly helpful for when someone might not identify with a specific label or identity.

Class position is particularly vulnerable for both us and our clients to approach. The influence of class on interpersonal sizing up, markers, and assumptions, as well as the quality of services associated with class are rarely acknowledged explicitly. Nor do we have the language to facilitate this conversation across social classes. Yet, avoidance of such a topic does not mean that it is absent in the therapeutic space. Transparency of identities of privilege and devaluation is encouraged to be engaged in a way that does not shame the therapist or the client. It is certainly useful for us as therapists to reflect on what goes into the relative ease and difficulty with talking about our respective identities. Linda's identities that are different from us as psychologists, and those with which we have less experience, could become the preferred focus of therapy because of the limitations that arise out of differences of the client. Here in our clinical role, we can understand that self-disclosure may be awkward for Linda as well, and strategies can be implemented to make Linda feel comfortable in identity self-disclosure.

Therapists, in negotiating the intersectionality of identity with their client, may discuss with their client the varied facets of identity that are significant to them, and how those might fall along a spectrum, rather than choosing between two binary points (e.g., male or female, gay or straight), which is extremely limiting. Having focused on those key components of identity, the therapist and client may discuss the ways in which those components overlap, conflict, or otherwise interact with one another. It may be helpful to refer to a visual to explore the ways in which those aspects of identity interact with and between contexts as well.

Considerations for Teaching and Training

For novice practitioners, it can be challenging to address interlocking identities and their associated privileges and oppressions. The challenge for trainers is how to break down the complexity of intersectionality to make it understandable and useful so that it becomes the regular part of practice. A training model, GRACES (Butler, 2015), consolidates a multitude of potential identities into fifteen social categories and provides a scaffold. Trainees can explore biases on the grid through the inclusion of different aspects of identity related to case studies/hypothetical clients (Butler, 2015). In processing reactions to a case, trainees may find they have different reactions to the hypothetical client based on the intersection of identities; may focus more on those aspects of identity that they are more comfortable addressing; and may focus less on those aspects of identity that they are less familiar with. Trainers can help trainees identify where they may need to work to take risks in exploring controversial aspects of difference and how these privileges intersect in helpful and unhelpful ways with the lived experiences of a client's contexts.

Ratts (2017) published a tool to help with the identity conversation, beginning with therapists developing their own awareness of identity and privilege. To work effectively with diverse clients, it is important to address gaps in our own "incomplete consciousness." This helps us empathize and develop a greater awareness of our own privilege, which is associated with lower levels of prejudice. Another model used to examine various systemic influences and enhance an intersectional perspective is the ADDRESSING training model (Hays, 2016). ADDRESSING is an acronym whereby each letter represents a component of an individual's identity, each with its own associated cultural systems. The acronym stands for **A**ge and generational influences, **D**evelopmental and acquired **D**isabilities, **R**eligion and spiritual orientation, **E**thnicity, **S**ocioeconomic status, **S**exual orientation, **I**ndigenous heritage, **N**ational origin, and **G**ender (Hays, 2016). Trainees learn that each component of identity can hold certain privileges or marginalization, and a therapist's education, professional status, and other privileges can potentially serve as a barrier between their work as professionals and their clients. The ADDRESSING training model thus serves as a tool to consider the many facets of identity, as well as how each facet may contribute to ideas of privilege and power, contextual marginalization, and the therapeutic relationship.

Hays (2016) provides trainees an example of an older male client of Asian Indian heritage, indicating that far more knowledge of the client's contextual influences are necessary for effective treatment. The ADDRESSING model is used as a training example to develop several important questions we as the therapist may seek to answer, some of which include: What is his experience of disability? What is his gender and sexual orientation? What was his religious upbringing, and what are his current religious beliefs? What is his experience of cultural identity in an urban area where most non-Indians believe him to be Pakistani or Arab? What experience (if any) does he have with immigration? Being able to answer these questions not only gives us a deepened understanding of our client's contextual influences and identities, it also lays the groundwork for beginning to understand how these influences and identities might intersect to contribute to the client's experience of life. For example, being an older male may be of particular privilege in his home or heritage culture, while older adults are less valued in the United States. The same component of identity thus can be both an advantage and a disadvantage, depending on the context. Further exploration of identity may find certain components at odds with one another, or with us as the therapist. Trainees learn that taking time to examine intersecting identities is critical then for getting a sense of the client and how we can build a therapeutic relationship with that individual (Hays, 2016).

Considerations for Research

Research historically requires that individuals are categorized in socially constructed demographic categories, often separating and limiting identities. When studying intersectionality, it is important to consider who is included in a social category, allowing for intersectional diversity in a study's inclusion criteria. In an LGBTQ+ study, are lesbian women and gay men who are also bisexual intentionally included? Are international students from cultures that highly stigmatize homosexuality included? Are LGBTQ+ people who are poor included? If not, could the complexity of internalized homophobia or self-shaming be researched accurately? Furthermore, research articles habitually focus on only one component of identity. For example, 85% of articles focused on participants in the LGBTQ+ community neglected to mention race or ethnicity (Hope & Chappell, 2015); similarly, in a 15-year review of research, only 39% discussed race, class, and gender as integrated, and only 1.9% focused primarily on the integration of these intersecting identities (Ratts, 2017). As such, there is yet little empirical precedence for adopting an intersectional approach.

An example of an intersectional approach in research was outlined in Cole (2009). Cole referred to a study of Asian Indian immigrant women who contrasted their values and behavior with those of White women, whom they saw as "sexually promiscuous, lacking family orientation, and corrupted by feminism" (Cole, 2009, p. 174). An intersectional transnational feminist researcher would discuss this finding of difference between Asian Indian immigrant women and U.S. women as women of color creating an idealized gendered immigrant identity in attempts to protest immigrant discrimination in the U.S. and to save face of their heritage identity. In their culturally defensive position, the immigrant women are perhaps displacing the "divide and rule" oppression of colonialism, about which they are aware from the history of colonial India. Ironically, the participants' ancestors in India were victimized by British colonists' two-century suppression by splitting regional people and kingdoms, turning them against each other. British imperialists finally partitioned India into various countries, divided by religion and race.

Intersectionality research focuses on the dynamics of power in multiple contexts and systems that shape and limit the different levels of agency an individual person possesses. We are in a position to understand dynamics of power because our research includes the study of relationships-- human and systemic. For those of us engaged (or planning to be engaged) in intersectional research, it can be liberating as intersectionality promotes the importance of including greater depth and more perspectives within research conceptualization itself, thereby leading to more questions in the methodology. In addition, the discussion of results about relationships are more nuanced as we try to understand different contexts. For example, an individual who identifies as Black/African American and as a woman not only represents both contexts, but also represents their own third context. Ultimately, research on intersectionality helps us become more critical consumers of knowledge and place results into sharper relief.

Intersectionality poses the argument that individuals have different ideas about what their contexts mean to them and psychologists are able to study these individual responses. This can be done according to a rubric that addresses multiple contexts regarding identities and gives examples constructed to understand their intersectionality (Cole, 2009). For example, when researchers explore womanhood, if they attend to rubrics that promote the diversity within their research participants and include diverse cultural groups in the study, the very definition of what it means to be a woman in a society can be broadened (Grabe & Else-Quest, 2012). In other words, we can become more aware of what details to attend to in our studies that will help underrepresented groups in society feel heard. As researchers we can continue to approach complex topics such as identity conflict within groups with more questions derived from intersectionality conceptualization.

Qualitative methods can provide a more complex picture of intersectional lived experiences in contrast to research protocols that involve the completion of questionnaires. The additive approach that posits that social inequality increases with each additional stigmatized identity is antithetical to the theoretical fidelity of intersectionality because people's experiences are not conceptualized as discrete, independent, and summative (Bowleg, 2008). Similarly, the option "check all that apply" is an additive approach.

Consideration for Consultation

As psychologists, we can carry the power of being change agents in our respective occupations. Intersectionality psychologists have become activists, identifying social justice interventions for marginalized and subjugated social groups and leading coalitions against systemic operations of power and privilege. As consultants, we can help our organizational clients understand the importance of self-definition as well as the complexity of intersectional reference group identities within their membership and the consumers they serve. We can work within organizational contexts to help organizations understand their role in institutional racism and structural oppression. We consult on normative unconscious processes (Layton, 2006) to describe the psychological consequences of leading an organization where norms are constructed to maintain the status quo. At the center of normative unconscious processes is psychological splitting. Institutions benefit those in power by idealizing certain attributes while devaluing others--that is, splitting human capacities and attributes (e.g., responsible versus lazy/cutting corners) and attaching them to dominant and minority racial group members of the institution.

Consultants can elaborate that when splitting occurs in institutions, minority group members may devalue their self by enacting scenarios whereby they deemphasize, deny, or repress their oppression and inflate an identity of privilege to prevent themselves from knowing the feeling of oppression. Or, they may manage their anger associated with their oppression with displacement or projection of their own discriminatory beliefs towards others, both majority and marginalized groups (e.g., lateral violence). Those in the institution who are favored with structural privileges and are accustomed to entitlement may even recognize disproportionate systemic treatments, but resolve their anxiety or inner conflict by attributing societal inequalities to the inferiority of oppressed people (perceived as not hard working or not being timely). Or those who are less consciously aware of their privilege may collude with oppressive systems and even turn against the oppressed. However, when informed about intersectionality by the consulting psychologist, institutional leaders learn that the dichotomization of people into opponent identities may be less real than members of institutions being both oppressed (e.g., women) and privileged (e.g., with particular occupational skills) in different systemic structures and gaining strengths (e.g., advocacy leadership) where oppression and privilege meet.

Conclusion

As mental health professionals, we can help to liberate individuals through the development of self-definition. As psychologists who hold the honor of being able to assist individuals in the empowering process of positive self-definition; we are encouraged to explore the dynamic nature of identities; consider the connections of identities in personal, community, and societal contexts; and to delve into the intersections of privilege and oppression within and across these contexts. Such endeavors also require that we as psychologists develop the ability to understand our own identities and the interactional process of these identities with our clients. In addition, we can consider the ways in which intersectional perspectives can be included within research, training, and consultation. It is through this understanding of a fluid, intersectional identity that we can develop a truly multiculturally and holistically informed psychological practice.

References

Alegría, M., Canino, G., Shrout, P. E., Woo, M., Duan, N., Vila, D., Torres, M., Chen, C., & Meng, X. (2008). Prevalence of mental illness in immigrant and non-immigrant U.S. Latino groups. American Journal of Psychiatry, 165(3), 359-369. https://doi.org/10.1176/appi.ajp.2007.07040704

American Psychological Association (2017) Multicultural guidelines: An ecological approach to context, identity, and intersectionality. http://www.apa.org/about/policy/multicultural-guidelines.aspx

Bowleg, L. (2008). When Black + lesbian + woman ≠ Black lesbian woman: The methodological challenges of qualitative and quantitative intersectionality research. Sex Roles, 59(5-6), 312-325. https://doi.org/10.1007/s11199-008-9400-z

Brownstone, L. M., Holliman, B. D., Gerber, H. R., & Monteith, L. L. (2018). The phenomenology of military sexual trauma among women veterans. Psychology of Women Quarterly, 42(4), 399-413. https://doi.org/10.1177/0361684318791154

Buchanan, N. T., Settles, I. H., & Woods, K. C. (2008). Comparing sexual harassment subtypes among black and white women by military rank: Double jeopardy, the Jezebel, and the cult of true womanhood. Psychology of Women Quarterly, 32(4), 347-361. https://doi.org/10.1111/j.1471-6402.2008.00450.x

Burkard, A. W., & Knox, S. (2004). Effect of therapist color-blindness on empathy and attributions in cross-cultural counseling. Journal of Counseling Psychology, 51(4), 387-397. https://doi.org/10.1037/0022-0167.51.4.387

Butler, C. (2015). Intersectionality in family therapy training: Inviting students to embrace the complexities of lived experience. Journal of Family Therapy, 37(4), 583-589. https://doi.org/10.1111/1467-6427.12090

Cho, S., Crenshaw, K. W., & McCall, L. (2013). Toward a Field of intersectionality studies: Theory, applications, and praxis. Signs: Journal of Women in Culture and Society, 38(4), 785-810. https://doi.org/10.1086/669608

Clough, P. T., & Fine, M. (2007). Activism and pedagogies: Feminist reflections. Women's Studies Quarterly, 35, 255-275. http://www.jstor.org/stable/27649713

Cokley, K. O. (2002). Testing cross's revised racial identity model: An examination of the relationship between racial identity and internalized racialism. Journal of Counseling Psychology, 49(4), 476-483. https://doi.org/10.1037/0022-0167.49.4.476

Cole, E. R. (2009). Intersectionality and research in psychology. American Psychologist, 64(3), 170-180. https://doi.org/10.1037/a0014564

Cuthbert, K. (2019). "When we talk about gender we talk about sex": (A)sexuality and (A)gendered Subjectivities. Gender & Society, 33(6), 841-864. https://doi.org/10.1177/0891243219867916

Dardis, C. M., Reinhardt, K. M., Foynes, M. M., Medoff, N. E., & Street, A. E. (2018). "Who are you going to tell? Who's going to believe you?". Psychology of Women Quarterly, 42(4), 414-429. https://doi.org/10.1177/0361684318796783

Dawson, M., McDonnell, L., & Scott, S. (2016). Negotiating the boundaries of intimacy: The personal lives of asexual people. The Sociological Review, 64(2), 349-365. https://doi.org/10.1111/1467-954x.12362

Dee Watts-Jones, T. (2010). Location of self: Opening the door to dialogue on intersectionality in the therapy process. Family Process, 49(3), 405-420. https://doi.org/10.1111/j.1545-5300.2010.01330.x

Erikson, E. H. (1968). Identity: Youth and crisis.

Ginter, E. J., Roysircar, G., & Gerstein, L. H. (2018). Theories and applications of counseling and psychotherapy: Relevance across cultures and settings. SAGE Publications.

Grabe, S., & Else-Quest, N. M. (2012). The role of transnational feminism in psychology. Psychology of Women Quarterly, 36(2), 158-161. https://doi.org/10.1177/0361684312442164

Grzanka, P. R. (2014). Intersectionality: A foundations and frontiers reader. Westview Press.

Hays, P. A. (2016). Understanding clients' identities and contexts. Addressing cultural complexities in practice: Assessment, diagnosis, and therapy (3rd ed.), 79-99. https://doi.org/10.1037/14801-005

Helms, J. E. (1995). An update on Helms' White and People of Color racial identity models. In J.G. Ponterotto, J.M. Casas, L.A. Suzuki, & C.M. Alexander (Eds.), Handbook of multicultural counseling (2nd ed., pp. 143-192). SAGE.

Helms, J. E., & Cook, D. A. (1999). Using race and culture
        in counseling and psychotherapy: Theory and
        process. Pearson College Division.
Hope, D. A., & Chappell, C. L. (2015). Extending training
        in multicultural competencies to include individuals
        identifying as lesbian, gay, and bisexual: Key
        choice points for clinical psychology training
        programs. Clinical Psychology: Science and
        Practice, 22(2), 105-
        118. https://doi.org/10.1111/cpsp.12099
Hurtado, S., Alvarado, A. R., & Guillermo-Wann, C.
        (2015). Thinking about race: The salience of racial
        identity at two- and four-year colleges and the
        climate for diversity. The Journal of Higher
        Education, 86(1), 127-
        155. https://doi.org/10.1080/00221546.2015.117773
        59
Jenkins, S. R. (1996). Self-definition in thought action, and
        life path choices. Personality and Social Psychology
        Bulletin, 22(1), 99-
        111. https://doi.org/10.1177/0146167296221010
Kendi, I. X. (2019). How to be an antiracist. One
        World/Ballantine.
Kuperminc, G. P., Blatt, S. J., Shahar, G., Henrich, C., &
        Leadbeater, B. J. (2004). Cultural equivalence and
        cultural variance in longitudinal associations of
        young adolescent self-definition and interpersonal
        relatedness to psychological and school
        adjustment. Journal of Youth and
        Adolescence, 33(1), 13-
        30. https://doi.org/10.1023/a:1027378129042
Layton, L. (2006). Racial identities, racial enactments, and
        normative unconscious processes. The
        Psychoanalytic Quarterly, 75(1), 237-
        269. https://doi.org/10.1002/j.2167-
        4086.2006.tb00039.x

Morgenroth, T., & Ryan, M. K. (2020). The effects of
        gender trouble: An integrative theoretical
        framework of the perpetuation and disruption of the
        gender/Sex binary. Perspectives on Psychological
        Science,
        174569162090244. https://doi.org/10.1177/1745691
        620902442

Moshman, D. (2007). Social identity and its
        discontents. Journal of Applied Developmental
        Psychology, 28(2), 184-
        187. https://doi.org/10.1016/j.appdev.2006.12.006

Onwuachi-Willig, A. (2018, June 18). What about
        #UsToo?: The invisibility of race in the #MeToo
        movement. The Yale Law
        Journal. https://www.yalelawjournal.org/forum/wha
        t-about-ustoo

Ratts, M. J. (2017). Charting the center and the margins:
        Addressing identity, marginalization, and privilege
        in counseling. Journal of Mental Health
        Counseling, 39(2), 87-
        103. https://doi.org/10.17744/mehc.39.2.01

Ristock, J., Zoccole, A., Passante, L., & Potskin, J. (2017).
        Impacts of colonization on Indigenous two-
        spirit/LGBTQ Canadians' experiences of migration,
        mobility and relationship
        violence. Sexualities, 22(5-6), 767-
        784. https://doi.org/10.1177/1363460716681474

Roysircar, G. (2004). Cultural self-awareness assessment:
        Practice examples from psychology
        training. Professional Psychology: Research and
        Practice, 35(6), 658-
        666. https://doi.org/10.1037/0735-7028.35.6.658

Roysircar, G. (2009). The big picture of advocacy: Counselor, heal society and thyself. Journal of Counseling & Development, 87(3), 288-294. https://doi.org/10.1002/j.1556-6678.2009.tb00109.x

Sellers, R. M., Smith, M. A., Shelton, J. N., Rowley, S. A., & Chavous, T. M. (1998). Multidimensional model of racial identity: A reconceptualization of African American racial identity. Personality and Social Psychology Review, 2(1), 18-39. https://doi.org/10.1207/s15327957pspr0201_2

Tajfel, H. (1982). Social psychology of intergroup relations. Annual Review of Psychology, 33(1), 1-39. https://doi.org/10.1146/annurev.ps.33.020182.000245

Trimble, J. E., & Dickson, R. (2005). Ethnic gloss. In C. B. Fisher & R. M. Lerner, (Eds.), Encyclopedia of applied developmental science (Vol. 1, pp. 412–415). SAGE.

Vares, T. (2018). 'My [asexuality] is playing hell with my dating life': Romantic identified asexuals negotiate the dating game. Sexualities, 21(4), 520-536. https://doi.org/10.1177/1363460717716400

Chapter 3: Advocacy: The Case of an Indigenous Indian Adolescent

As psychology professionals, we recognize that oppression shapes negative outcomes for people and consider its role in causing disparities and disproportionalities in educational and mental health systems. Using an ecological framework, we can identify how interactions between larger cultural norms and societal laws resulting from privilege or oppression limit an individual's access to resources at individual and community levels. With this knowledge, we cannot only address disparities at individual level, but work to create change and advocate on systemic levels.

Mental health disparity is defined as "a significant [difference] in the overall rate of mental illness incidence or prevalence, morbidity, mortality or survival rates in a health disparity population as compared with the health status of the general population" (Safran et al., 2009, p. 1962). To address disparities, potential applications in practice, research, teaching/training, and consultation are suggested. The recommendations for solutions to inequity are based on theories of oppression, structural stigma, cultural stigma, cultural mistrust, and social capital, as well as based upon the implications of social justice action that works to translate the voice of psychology into public policy.

The following case illustration is used to help demonstrate the ways in which an ecological understanding of oppression can inform clinical practice, teaching, research, and consultation.

Case Illustration-- Darryl

Darryl is a 16-year-old, American Indian boy from a reservation near Oklahoma City in the United States. His passions include music, soccer, and academics. He presents to therapy in a community mental health center located in a nearby city. He recently moved in with his uncle, aunt, and cousins in order to attend a better school. His aim for seeking help is for support with adjusting to his primarily White/White American school in the city and feelings of shame and guilt over his decision to leave his reservation.

Growing up, Darryl describes life on the reservation as difficult. Many of his neighbors and family members experienced alcoholism and extreme poverty. Darryl remembers never having enough money for food, healthcare, transportation, or adequate clothing and shoes. His father is an alcoholic and his mother used to be one. Darryl says that his parents are both intelligent and talented, but that they did not have the opportunities to pursue school or career interests. He described feeling pressure to be successful in the ways in which his parents were not. He appreciates how tight knit his community and family are but also acknowledges how a loss of culture, opportunity, and a satisfying life has embittered them.

Darryl was born with a cleft pallet, which has affected his facial and dental appearance. He said that it also contributed to multiple ear infections as a child, and that he has partial hearing loss in one of his ears because of unmanaged issues. He reports that his physical appearance has been the cause of a lot of bullying, both verbal and physical (e.g., getting "beat up" often). Darryl had some friendships, but they faded when Darryl had an opportunity to transfer to another school off the reservation. Darryl said that many of the students at his current school are judgmental of the school on the reservation, and that they assume his prior education was poor. He also speculates they assume he is dumb because of his appearance and partial loss of hearing. Darryl shared he had felt stifled by the lack of academic opportunities on the reservation, and he worried that he was not being set up to be a competitive college candidate.

Darryl continued to be bullied at this new school. As the only American Indian, students called him American Indian racist names and made racist jokes to his face. Even the teachers assumed he was unintelligent. Darryl said that he tried to ignore the comments, as his teachers and parents advised. Although it took him a while to connect with his White/White American classmates, eventually Darryl was able to make friends.

As he settled in his White majority school, Darryl felt like he was losing his Indian identity. He experienced shunning from his tribe after his decision to attend school outside the reservation, and he was frequently called White racist names by his old friends. Balancing his loyalties to his tribe, himself, and his academic dreams had become a struggle.

Darryl shares in therapy that he feels immense guilt for befriending White/White American students, who had once made racist comments to him and towards his tribe. He said that he is both grateful for the educational opportunity, but he feels disloyal to students receiving a poor education on the reservation. He said that he would like to feel better about these things as he starts to think about applying to colleges and possibly leaving the area entirely.

Personal Reflection Questions

- What feelings do you notice coming up as you read about Darryl? How might these feelings support your understanding of Darryl versus how might your feelings be an interpretation of how you imagine Darryl himself feels?
- What immediate thoughts are coming to mind? Do you notice yourself asking questions that are based in trying to determine a diagnosis or treatment? What would it be like to focus on understanding Darryl's story and experience?

- What are the systemic similarities and differences between American Indian reservations and U.S. Federal Land? How are they governed and funded? How do I imagine governmental controls affect those who live on reservations?

Discussion Questions Related to Darryl

- What would you identify as some of the key themes that Darryl is struggling with?
- What are some of the adolescent developmental issues that Darryl is experiencing?
- How can these adolescent developmental issues be understood within the context of the Darryl's reference groups?
- How would you work with Darryl to help him manage the intersectionality of his identities (American Indian-White/White American, low class-privileged class, ability-disability, etc.)?
- How would you build trust in your counseling relationship with Darryl?
- How would you support Darryl's efforts to maintain his identity as an American Indian and stay connected with his community?

Literature Review

Oppression is described as when one group possesses greater access to power and privilege than another group, and when the said inequity is used to uphold the dominance of one group over the other (David, 2014). Figure 2 presents a visual depiction of an ecological model that includes macrolevel oppression and microlevel disparities. Utilizing Bronfenbrenner's ecological nested model, this figure is an illustration of hierarchical and interactive process of systems that cause disparities in law, justice, and healthcare. This

Figure 2. *An Ecological Model of Macrolevel Oppression and Microlevel Disparities*

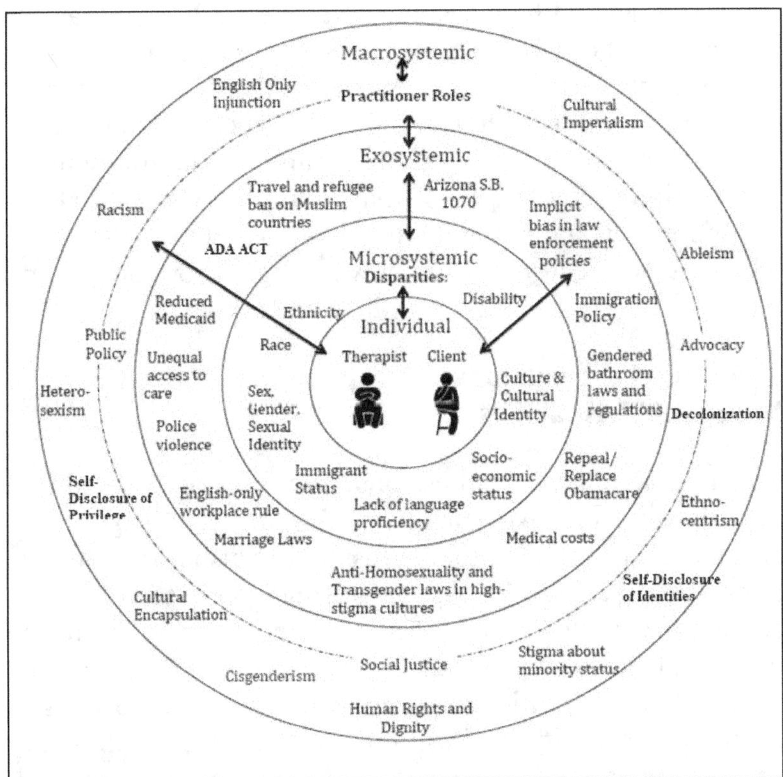

Note: A visual depiction of an ecological model that includes macrolevel oppression and microlevel disparities.

figure shows that we are in constant contact with the societal structures and institutions that surround us. These include ways of understanding the world at the macrolevel, such as entitlement, privilege, oppression, sexism, racism, and classism, and related policies and practices at the exosystemic level. As psychology professionals in the community, involved at the microsystemic level, we engage with multiple institutions, including those specific to our place of work (e.g., community mental health centers, hospitals, schools, etc.), those that have direct involvement with our patients' care (e.g., Parole Board, Department of Child Protective Services, Department of Disability Services, etc.), and those that influence our patients' ability at the individual-interpersonal level to receive care (e.g., insurance companies). The following literature review details what we mean by structural oppression and cultural stigma and how these lead to disparities. We also discuss how a religious orientation in healthcare can reduce disparities.

Macrolevel Structural Oppressions Leading to Microlevel Disparities

Macro level oppressions, such as racism, cultural imperialism, classism, ableism, English language only, cisgenderism, and sexism, result in disparities at the microsystemic level. As a result, oppressed people experience limited access, less utilization, and diminished quality of healthcare (Institute of Medicine, 2003). Below we illustrate disparities for American Indians in the areas of economic stability, education, social and community context, health and healthcare, and neighborhood and built environments.

American Indian (AI) tribal members in a study (Martin et al., 2016) endorsed Social Determinants of Health (SDOH), such as poverty, unemployment, limited resources, geographic isolation, along with difficulties in policy and political leadership. These contextual factors shaped both prevalence and perception of the disease of diabetes. SDOH factors are well regarded as contributing to poor mental health for racial and ethnic minorities but have been overlooked among AIs (Brondolo et al., 2017). The Centers for Disease Control and Prevention (2013) defined SDOH as the conditions and settings in which people live that affect a wide range of health, functioning, and quality-of-life outcomes and risks. Approximately 75% of the AI workforce earns less than $7,000 per year; in 2011, one quarter of American Indians and Alaska Natives (AI/AN) lived in poverty (Austin, 2013). In what has been described as the painful legacy of discrimination, in 2009-2011 the employment rate of AIs was 64.7% (25-54 years of age) in comparison to 78.1 % of White/White Americans (The White House Office of the Press Secretary 2013; Austin, 2013). Unemployment rates on some reservations are as high as 90% (Garrett et al., 2012). In many areas, arrest rates for American Indians are three times those for Blacks/African Americans (Garrett et al., 2012).

AI youth have the lowest educational attainment rates in the country. In 2010, only 69% of AIs finished high school in comparison to the 80% nationwide average (Norris et al., 2012). Further, only 17% of AI youth continue from high school to college in comparison to 60% of high school students nationwide (Norris et al., 2012). Much of the housing is inadequate and substandard. On the Navajo reservation, for example, 46% of residents have no electricity, 54% have no indoor plumbing, and 82% live without a telephone (Garrett et al., 2012). Therefore, by keeping this information in mind to help provide a specific context for the struggle that many Native people face in day-to-day living, it is also important to understand the historical context and stories that are involved in this struggle for survival for many (Garrett et al., 2012). There are also problems with affordable housing, as illustrated by the following quotation:

> Yeah, cause I know like people who appear
> as a visible minority, especially when they're
> Aboriginal, like if they sound Aboriginal on
> the phone, they don't get the call back . . .
> [Also] like I know a lot of landlords get really

upset if they figure out that, like those two roommates aren't roommates, you know. (Me´ tis, Two-Spirit, bisexual, queer, female, 20s, Winnipeg). (Ristock et al., 2017, p. 779)

Based on available data for 2006, AI adults (specifically, those reporting one race) experienced the highest rates of both psychological distress (25.9%) and Major Depressive Episode (12.1%) in comparison to the general adult population (Urban Indian Health Institute, 2012). AIs also reported lifetime prevalence of drug use disorders as 18.4%, compared to 10.3% for the total population (American Psychiatric Association [APA], 2010). Based on data from the 2014 National Survey on Drug Use and Health, past-year substance abuse rates for AIs were 16% as compared to non-Hispanic White (8%), non-Hispanic Black (8.6%), Hispanic (8.5%), Asian (4.5%), and Native Hawaiian or other Pacific Islanders (10%) (Bagalman & Heisler, 2016). As of 2010, PTSD was twice as likely among AI individuals as compared to the general population (APA, 2010). Bagalman and Heisler (2016) found that PTSD and suicidal behavior occurred at higher rates among AIs than all other racial-ethnic groups assessed. Rates of mental health disorder for AI's are often higher among those living in reservation-based areas and among IA women although unique disparities exist (see Beals et al., 2005 for a two-tribe comparison by gender).

Growing up in poverty can create strain for children and their families, and AI children experience a significant amount of Adverse Childhood Experiences (ACES). Utilizing the National Survey of Children's Health, Kenney and Singh (2016) found that AI children 17 years of age or younger were far more likely to have had 8 out of 9 ACEs, including neglect, witnessing, or experiencing violent victimization, household substance abuse, domestic violence, parental incarceration, and divorce. In addition, "discrimination and the memory of historical trauma work in tandem to add immeasurably to the inherent difficulties in the development of children who live on reservations" (Brockie et al., 2015, p. 418). Historical trauma is conceptualized as a complex trauma inflicted upon a group with shared identity, affiliation, or circumstance over time (Mohatt et al., 2014). This trauma is believed to be transmitted across generations, and it may greatly impact family and community systems by disrupting natural supports through loss of cultural mechanisms like traditional parenting practices and healthy displays of parental warmth (Mohatt et al., 2014).

In one study, AIs explained that their contemporary problems' etiology was in traumatic events known as the "soul wound" (Duran et al., 1998). This "soul wound" has been described as historical trauma, historical legacy, the AI holocaust, and intergenerational posttraumatic stress disorder (Duran et al., 1998). This "cumulative racial trauma can leave scars for those who are dehumanized" (Comas-Díaz et al., 2019, p. 1). In addition, understanding historical trauma allows us to conceptualize discriminatory policies as trauma cues to the community. When the community experiences such reminders, it and its members are likely to be affected. If a frequency of incidences of discrimination significantly predicts posttraumatic stress disorder diagnostic status (Tucker et al., 2015), and these communities are continuously experiencing discrimination through policy, we must take seriously the incredible influence of discriminatory policy on community and individual mental health. Thus, it is imperative that psychology professionals do not ignore the impact of historical trauma (Gone et al., 2019).

As a caution, when reporting statistics with such strong implications for deviation from healthy mental functioning, researchers run the risk of pathologizing AI peoples. Indeed, AI peoples have long been the subjects of research that ignores the intersectional nature of psychosocial dimensions and ecological risk factors among AI communities in favor of deficit-based approaches with pathological foci. An understanding of the contexts and histories in which Native peoples are situated is crucial to understanding AI mental health. At the same time, access to mental health care is absolutely integral in alleviating the effects of mental health disparity in AI communities due to substantial contextual risk factors (Gone & Trimble, 2012).

In the last decade, research has described broad, structural forms of stigma. These forms of stigma speak to how stereotypes and biases can establish themselves within an institution's culture, ways of understanding the world, policies, and procedures. Thus, such analysis allows us to recognize the ways in which systems themselves are structured to create disparities. Expanding the stigma construct beyond individual and microsystemic levels to macrosocial forms allows psychology professionals to establish larger models of societal dynamics and their social, emotional, and political impact on groups and individuals, as illustrated by the chapter's case vignette and literature review on American Indians.

Structural stigma is often intentional. Intentional structural stigma is typically manifested as rules, policies, and procedures of exolevel entities in positions of power (Corrigan et al., 2004). One cross-national study focused on the way the combination of national legislation (ban against homosexuality) and social attitudes (heteronormativity) were linked to specific stigmatization processes at community and individual levels for sexual minority individuals (Pachankis et al., 2015). This study showed that sexual minority men were more likely to conceal their sexual orientation and/or gender identity in countries that were determined to have high levels of structural stigma as compared to low stigma countries. The implication of this is that institutional structures do not simply impact the services that one receives but goes as deep as to influence the ways in which an individual's identity can co-exist within a system.

As applied to Darryl, his American Indian reservation has been structurally marginalized by White/White American inequitable policies in education, employment, healthcare/dental care, and social support. These policies not only create disparity but continue a legacy of colonization. According to Buchwald et al. (2000), family, access to education, and resources for expressing spiritual/religious needs were viewed by AIs as assets that created a support network for themselves and their families when faced with health disparity. Disenfranchisement from traditionally rooted methods of health and healing, stemming from colonization and the resulting diaspora, greatly impacts the ability to tend to health both physically and mentally. Through disenfranchisement from traditional practices, many AIs have little or no outlet for understanding or effectively coping with cumulative adverse effects (Buchwald et al., 2000).

Cultural Stigma

Stigma can be located within a culture. Psychotherapy with AI populations may pose challenges because many AIs view counseling with suspicion (Turner & Pope, 2009). It has been suggested that AIs believe that the construct of mental illness has been imposed on them by Whites/White Americans, and that mental health treatment is a potential form of social control that parallels the social control established by centuries of legislative injustices in past generations (Turner & Pope, 2009). For many AIs, there is stigma also attached to alcohol abuse, substance abuse, and other mental illnesses, so they may be reluctant to stay in treatment (Turner & Pope, 2009). Today, community engagement and ceremony (e.g., powwows, stomp dances) are the most accessible means of traditional healing (Manson, 2000). Also, AIs are far less likely to have private insurance and may rely solely on Indian Health Services and tribal clinics for behavioral health needs (Buchwald et al., 2000). As such, there is an understandable and considerable push to "make the most" of behavioral health services in Indian Country. It makes sense to look at mechanisms that underlie multiple diagnoses, which allow providers to do the most good, with the least amount of resources, to address disparate rates of mental health disorder for AI peoples (Buchwald et al., 2000).

In Darryl's case, he must balance his community's distrust alongside his desire for a good education, his moving away from his reservation, and his criticism of the abuse and alcoholism in his family and tribespeople. Rather than feeling connected to the intersectionality of two cultures, he appears to be stigmatized by both. He also may question whether he has internalized a stigma toward his own culture, and if that has motivated his choices. Briefly, internalized oppression, is defined as when oppressed racial and ethnic minority people promote White/White American dominance or the devaluation of marginalized societies through acts of horizontal/lateral oppression against their own people, which has been argued to be the most harmful psychological effect of oppression (Speight, 2007). Such experiences could lead to Darryl feeling disconnected and guilty.

The above-mentioned Indigenous American experiences must not only be considered and included, but actively integrated into research, teaching, and practice (Adams, et al., 2017). Similarly, the experiences and viewpoints of groups must be understood as flexible and evolving, rather than stagnant. Oversimplifying a group or culture to one viewpoint or feature, however representative at one point in time, continues to perpetuate misunderstanding and misrepresentation. Ristock et al. (2017) write about how allowing research participants to self-identify allows for visibility and can contribute to deviations from colonized demographics.

Religious Orientation

The United States is a society that prides itself on freedom of religion. However, in the attempt to keep this freedom for all and not impinge upon the rights of others, individuals become uncomfortable speaking about religion (Mitchum, 2012). Although primary care is seeing more of a return to mind-body connections, religion has generally not been a part of U.S. medical practices. When religion and spirituality are integrated into medical care, it is often for palliative care rather than for health promotion (Isaac et al., 2016). The same holds true for psychology--with religion and faith not necessarily being a consideration in psychological work. Religion can influence how people understand their illness (Diefenbach & Leventhal, 1996), can have an impact on medical decisions (Koenig, 2012), and can influence one's emotional experience (Herzig et al., 2013; Padela & Curlin, 2012).

There is a lack of training in the field of psychology on the role of religion and spirituality in treatment even though approximately 90% of the world's population has spiritual beliefs that are essential to their coping (Pargament et al., 1998). This training is particularly important, given research that indicates the impact of religion and spirituality on health behaviors can influence both positive and negative health outcomes (Isaac et al., 2016, Pargament et al., 1998). Community-based interventions that have actively involved faith-based communities in health promotion have been found to lead to positive behavioral outcomes (Roysircar et al., 2019b).

With regard to AIs, the essence of spirituality is the feeling of connection, which is available to everyone, although experienced in different ways (Garrett et al., 2012).

AIs generally believe that human beings are made up of spirit, mind, and body, which are all interconnected; therefore, illness affects the mind, body, and spirit all together. Wellness is considered to be the harmony of mind, body, and spirit, with "unwellness" being disharmony, as experienced by Darryl in this chapter's case vignette (Garrett et al., 2012). Natural unwellness is caused by the violation of a sacred social or natural law of creation (e.g., participating in a sacred ceremony while under the influence of alcohol, drugs, or having had sex within four days of the ceremony), and unnatural unwellness is caused by conjuring witchcraft from those with destructive intentions. Each person is responsible for their own wellness by keeping attuned to self, relations, the environment, and the universe (Garrett et al., 2012). These spiritual beliefs provide insight into some of the values held by traditional AI clients and could be useful when considering diagnosis and treatment. Psychology professionals also understand that spiritual beliefs depend on a variety of factors such as acculturation, geographic region, family structure, religious influences, and tribal-specific traditions.

Considerations for Clinical Practice

Much of the work in mental health service surrounds the treatment itself (e.g., multicultural competence or evidence-based practice) rather than a focus on issues of accessibility. One inherent challenge to accessing mental health care in low income and cultural minority communities is a lack of awareness of resources or how resources can help. It is also likely that seeking psychological services is simply not within the realm of a difficult everyday life. On the other hand, learning about what therapy provides, what a therapist's role entails, what a client's role entails, how change occurs, and how one might benefit from a therapist's social-emotional support may be necessary for a community to access treatment. The responsibility, therefore, resides in us as clinicians to find ways and means to inform and educate localities where services are less likely to be accessed.

Accessibility

To support access to mental health services, psychological professionals can create programs that address accessibility on multiple levels. We might engage in education and outreach efforts for diverse communities to help de-stigmatize help seeking, reduce limitations on service utilization, and build collaborative relationships with the stakeholders of communities (Roysircar, 2013). Such efforts can begin wide, with open informal groups offering a free and useful service that would help initially to draw community members to a clinic. For example, providing play groups for young children that offer parenting support, education, and socializing might be useful as caregivers may form trusting and familiar relationships with those at the clinic (Roysircar et al., 2019b). This, in turn, may increase the likelihood that caretakers will feel comfortable accessing psychological services for their children and their families in the future. Such open community groups may also serve to normalize mental health services in neighborhoods where native knowledge and culture would not typically draw people to a mental health clinic.

Ableism

Darryl also has a disability, and he is likely to be negatively impacted by ableism. Ableism is the persistent marginalization and devaluation of people based on a perceived deficit in physical or mental ability (Lalvani & Bacon, 2018). People with disabilities have historically been excluded from mainstream society, which has perpetuated the false perception that they are unable to participate in mainstream society (Harpur, 2009). This belief has been sustained despite approximately 25.7% of the U.S. noninstitutionalized adult population identifying with one or more disabilities (Smith et al., 2020). Ableism overlooks barriers to education, information, occupation, physical space, and social spaces that often impact people with disabilities.

Ableism is often under-identified because of indirect discrimination. Direct discrimination is when a discriminator focuses on the person's disability, while indirect discrimination excludes people using what seems to be neutral policy (Harpur, 2009). For example, a gym might not have a policy that bans people with ambulatory issues from entering (which would be direct discrimination); however, the presence of stairs and lack of accessible parking (indirect discrimination) communicates a similar sentiment. In another example, websites might not state that visually impaired people are unwelcome to view content; however, a lack of Alt Text or image descriptions serves the same function.

People with disabilities are more likely to be unemployed, to live in poverty, and to rely on public insurance coverage than others (Smith et. al., 2020). In 2016, 34.8% of working-age people with disabilities in the U.S. had worked in the past year, and only 15.5% had worked 40 or more hours (Smith et al., 2020). This not only contributes to economic disparity, but often also translates to low access to healthcare, and can reinforce the idea that people with disabilities are unable or unwilling to work. People with disabilities are also likely to be seen as irresponsible, childlike, sad, burdensome, "evil villains" or "tragic victims" (Lalvani & Bacon, 2018; Smith et al., 2020).

People with disabilities are 1 to 1.5 times more likely than the national population to experience bullying, which can increase a student's risk for depression, suicide, feeling unsafe at school, and academic underachievement (Blake et al., 2016; Lalvani & Bacon, 2018). The three components of bullying include intent to harm, power imbalance, and repetition of acts, and bullying can happen physically, verbally, relationally, and through cyber methods (Cook et al., 2016). While friendships can help mitigate bullying, students with visible disabilities tend to be more excluded (Blake et al., 2016). Often, adults working with students who have disabilities encourage them to ignore the bullying, when this is the least helpful intervention (Lalvani & Bacon, 2018). Youths with disability might also lash out in self-preservation, which can place them in both "bully-victim" roles, and inadvertently contribute to more negative perceptions about people with disabilities. Both bullying and self-defensive behaviors can exacerbate social isolation during a pivotal social development phase (Blake et al., 2016).

For many, the bullying is not something that passes once they mature. Research supports that bullying often continues through adult years, although it manifests differently (Cook et al., 2016). Systemically, there are also issues when disability is not a federally protected factor (like in the case of older buildings with low accessibility), and some of the discrimination is indirect like inadequate restroom facilities (Harpur, 2009). Harpur (2009) argued that ableism needs to be addressed through a social justice model, in which people who marginalize others should be held accountable to change their practices and reduce barriers for people with disabilities.

Darryl described being bullied due to racism, physical appearance, and potentially due to hearing loss. It is also possible that Darryl has internalized ableism, and that he might not classify hurtful comments about his face as bullying to his therapist. Lavani and Bacon (2018) propose that young children with disabilities could benefit from a positive self-identity; however, it is unclear if and to what extend Darryl might have one about his disfigurement.

Similarly, Darryl might not identify as having a disability. He might see himself as an athlete and physically skilled. A psychology professional should not label Darryl's identities, but rather explore how he identifies and the effects of how others identify him.

Motivation and Retention Considerations

Milburn and Lightfoot (2016) found that family-based interventions for behavior changes in adolescents were successful when Latino/Hispanic/Latinx families were involved at every level of the intervention, particularly in the enrollment, engagement, and retention processes. Higher retention among Latino/Hispanic/Latinx families was linked to higher educational level and income. Millburn and Lightfoot (2016) also noted that there was an increased enrollment in a clinical research project for Latino/Hispanic/Latinx parents with less education when provided with an incentive, but the authors reported that these parents were less willing to participate once the study started. It is, therefore, important to consider utilization barriers and develop strategies that might enable parents to increase their levels of motivation and retention.

Historical Trauma

Suicide has had a disproportional impact on AI populations for over half a century. Despite their sufferings, AI youth often avoid psychological services and there appears to be a disconnect between school suicide prevention programs and AI communities because many interventions do not explicitly address cultural and colonization factors (LaFromboise & Malik, 2016), such as historical trauma. Lafromboise and Malik (2016) encourage discussions with AI groups to validate their fears and build relationships characterized by trust and understanding. Based on cultural and familial factors of an AI community, the Zuni Life Skills Development Curriculum is a suicide prevention intervention program "designed using a model of social cognitive development to remediate the behavioral and cognitive correlates of suicide" (LaFromboise & Howard-Pitney, 1995, p. 479). The Zuni curriculum was developed in collaboration with the Zuni pueblo and presented in its tribal high school. The model included factors that contribute to depression, demoralization, and trauma and raise AI/AN suicide rates; these factors were perceived discrimination and negative stereotypes, interpersonal/social issues of adolescence, historical trauma, acculturative stress, community violence, gang activity, substance use, and culturally oppressive policies (LaFromboise & Howard-Pitney, 1995). Students who participated in the curriculum had better scores on suicide probability and hopelessness, were better able to problem solve, and had better intervention skills regarding suicide in comparison to the control group (LaFromboise & Howard-Pitney, 1995). Such results suggest the importance of understanding and speaking to incorporating communities in collaborative efforts to promote positive mental health outcomes.

Possible Interventions

One therapeutic intervention that Darryl will likely benefit from is the use of externalization and framing of the problem within a sociohistorical context. The therapist and Darryl can work together on redefining the problem as something outside of Darryl and not an intrinsic part of who he is. For example, his experiences of racism and losses could be externalized and reframed within the larger sociohistorical context of oppression and genocide against AIs, instead of Darryl seeing himself as being deficient. Therefore, the therapist could work to help Darryl see the generational traumatic effects of having land stripped away, being forced to live on resource-scarce reservations, losing cultural traditions and heritage, and not having political power, and how these could contribute to high rates of alcoholism and poverty in his family and reservation (Turner & Pope, 2009). This logic could be applied to Darryl's personal life and how chains of negative historical events are related to why his White/White American classmates viewed him as "lesser" and to racial power dynamics. Externalization will also help Darryl see times in which there were "exceptions" to the sociohistorical rules when he had superseded the rules with hope. For example, he successfully attended a high-resourced school, joined a sports team, and made meaningful friendships.

We engage in cultural empathy as we consider cultural/community perspectives. Incorporating an American Indian healing perspective is a way to de-colonialize practice. One study found that to treat transgenerational and other trauma, listening to traditional music played on an American Indian flute led to integration of affect and memory, significant decreases in anxiety, and increases in perceptions of interconnectedness (Turner & Pope, 2009). In Native culture, stories, anecdotes, and witty one-liners are examples of an expression of the spirit. This tradition is uniquely observed in every tribal nation but shares the same power across tribes (Garrett et al., 2005). Along those same lines, humor is often used in therapy because humor is considered a spiritual tradition, a healing force. Garrett et al. (2005) stated that "the use of humor in counseling has been associated with increasing trust, reducing stress, promoting holistic wellness, creating needed perspective, boosting physiological well-being, and allowing clients to take control of their lives" (p. 195). The use of humor in therapy has been described as "a healthy way of feeling a 'distance' between one's self and the problem, a way of standing off and looking at one's problem with perspective" (Garrett et al., 2005, p. 196). Humor allows the therapist to convey a sense of genuineness and empathy to the client. Humor serves in helping persecuted groups deal with tragedy by giving them a means of poking fun at their oppressors. Laughing will take away a bully's power over Darryl, relieve his stress, and create an atmosphere of sharing and connectedness (Garrett et al., 2005). A major goal of using humor with Darryl is to help him become integrated and spontaneous in his relationships, as well as to learn helpful coping strategies.

Another useful intervention will be to utilize Darryl's love of drawing and writing to help him gain mastery over his problems. The therapist should encourage Darryl to draw and author representations of preferred storylines that exist beyond his problems. Darryl could be empowered to become an expert of his new life and story. American Indian tradition honors the power of the self to heal and right itself with the help of the environment, and the need for an alliance with the hope that life can get better (Garrett et al., 2012). This exercise could help discover what is truly important and intrinsic to Darryl and his happiness.

Finally, another intervention could be letter writing to his family. Darryl is in need of finding an appreciative audience to support him and help his new stories take root. Making relational connections is especially helpful for American Indians because family and community are valued. Darryl could share his new drawings and narratives in his letters to his family that explain his new perspective of his life and difficulties. By including his larger social network in his journey to reconceptualize his life, it is more likely that his new storyline will gain traction and credibility. Also, it may help Darryl become closer to his family and friend from whom he feels distant. With mutual understanding and open communication, it is hoped that connections will be augmented, and Darryl will find a support system to sustain his motivation to stay on the path of his new life.

Considerations for Teaching and Training

The concept of cultural mistrust refers to the idea that targets of oppression bring a justifiable skepticism to medical, mental health, and research settings due to prior exploitation. Validating clients' cultural mistrust and demonstrating cultural humility and a willingness to engage in open processing of racial issues can strengthen the therapeutic alliance and ultimately enhance treatment outcomes (Terrell & Terrell, 1984; Ward, 2002). Self-disclosure that is considered an essential component of positive therapy outcomes is affected by cultural mistrust. However, the process of self-disclosure is often minimally included in the culturally adapted interventions that trainees learn. Future training research can focus on the important aspects of self-disclosure and the therapeutic alliance when considering reasons why mental health services are not accessed and utilized widely within diverse communities.

Trainees need to develop critical consciousness. Freire's (1972) critical consciousness theory encompasses awareness of multiple forms of oppression including classism, racism, and heterosexism. Freire proposed that through critical consciousness about inequalities and injustice, people (like our clients) who are oppressed can become active agents working toward change. Indeed, research has linked critical consciousness to various indicators of empowerment, such as, social justice-oriented political participation (e.g., Parent & Silva, 2018). Although not grounded explicitly in Freire's theorizing, social psychological theories and research also point to critical consciousness about injustice as a predictor of collective action for change (e.g., for a review see van Zomeren et al., 2008). This notion is also captured in the feminist therapy guiding principle that the personal is political in systems of inequality that oppress women and in women's resistance against those systems (e.g., Brown, 2018).

Thanks to the success of endeavors of intentional mentorship and recruitment of more diverse graduate student cohorts, students of color accounted for 31.7% ($n = 1892$) of doctoral degrees in psychology awarded in 2016, up from 22.2% ($n = 978$) in 2006 (American Psychological Association [ApA] Center for Workforce Studies, 2017). Thus, admission disparity at the doctoral level of training in professional psychology is being reduced. However, a majority of the textbooks and teaching tools for developing multicultural competence continue to address students from dominant culture identities with the goal being to help them learn enough to not cause harm when working with diverse communities (Blackwell, 2010). Seward (2014) has noted pedagogical styles that focus on teaching White/White American students to be multiculturally competent, and in doing so, center the educational needs of dominant group member students, which is experienced as marginalizing to students of color and amounts to structural neglect of students of color. Logan and colleagues (2013) discussed this tension in teaching strategies regarding race by noting that "though it is fundamentally anti-racist and activist in nature, the fact that this literature tends to assume and center White racial subjects, means that, ironically, it also reproduces a kind of White privilege" (p. 124).

Considerations for Research

A practice of inclusion of communities into our research practice can hold us more responsible to communities we research, allows us to discover new ways of understanding a phenomenon from a community's perspective, and provides us with a more informed context with which to interpret results (Roysircar et al., 2017, 2019a). In addition, if we include those communities with which we research in our work, we shift systemic power structures, providing power to communities that have been historically misunderstood, misrepresented, or not represented by research (Roysircar et al. 2019b). When working with a community, an understanding of the historical context of research within that community is critical, as well. Recognizing how past researchers have engaged (or not engaged) with communities, acknowledges ways in which research may have decreased trust and promoted oppression or colonization.

We must also seek to increase our research on topics related to power, privilege, oppression, and inequities and their connections to institutions, systems, and services. For example, multicultural scholars have conceptualized the phenomenon of lateral violence—an interpersonal consequence of internalized oppression. One area of research is to explore the experience and impact of lateral violence.

Another example of research in these areas is from Carter (2007). Carter has proposed race-based traumatic stress as a form of oppression-based trauma and illustrates how this contextual trauma is derived from identity-based microaggressions against people of color. Carter's theory provides indirect support to test microaggressions against AIs, for example in educational settings, and a race-based traumatic stress hypothesis; however, research must specifically test this relationship. Carter has argued that race-based traumatic stress is separate from PTSD and is a unique form of psychological injury. Because of this, Carter developed a scale to assess the unique phenomena of race-based traumatic stress for Black/African Americans rather than assessing it with PTSD measures. Roysircar and colleagues (2017, 2019 a, b) have assessed trauma and resilience in children with their house, tree, and person drawings. Given Native peoples' interest in artwork, this creative activity can be used to assess their well-being.

Research is also lacking regarding access and utilization of mental health services. With regard to studies on refugee and immigrant mental health, much of this work focuses on specialist services like inpatient care and do not address the whole range of service sectors where mental healthcare is provided. Research is needed on access and utilization of services for refugee and immigrant children. Related to this, more research is needed on the experience of trauma and its impact on refugee children and their families and on unaccompanied minors and separated children placed in U.S. detention centers along the southwestern U.S. border. In taking a community-based approach to research, such investigations can explore how the service delivery system encourages or interferes with access to treatment.

Integrated health care research may further serve to increase access to care and destigmatize seeking mental healthcare among racial and ethnic minority, refugee, immigrant, and less privileged populations. From a meta-analytic perspective, such research should be dynamically focused on the multiple arenas of healthcare and service delivery, including access to and awareness of healthcare options, utilization of such options, responsiveness to cultural diversity with regard to healthcare missions, immigrant/refugee perceptions of the quality of obtainable healthcare options, and healthcare treatment outcomes for marginalized status individuals.

While literature focusing on mental healthcare in specific groups of immigrants, for example (Li & Seidman, 2010; Roberts et al., 2015), is important, comparative studies can provide us with information about dynamics related to different patterns of help seeking behaviors and how those patterns might influence access and utilization. Comparative studies that include marginalized and dominant groups might be utilized to better understand the disparities in mental healthcare between non-mainstream and mainstream help-seeking individuals. Similar studies have been conducted in international settings (e.g., Hollander et al., 2011), and findings showed disparities by race or immigrant/refugee status as well as by gender, age, socioeconomic status, and community support.

Considerations for Consultation

Awareness of one's privilege is critical for providing culturally competent care. Consulting with a group that is having interpersonal difficulties can facilitate discussions about the effects of a structurally imposed disparity, such as social class. Similarly, such discussions can facilitate consciousness of how group dynamics may reflect power dynamics in the larger society (Roysircar, 2008).

It is argued that the actions of psychological professionals extend beyond in-session treatment to a balanced recognition of client presentations due to systemic disparities and unique individual characteristics of a client. Therefore, per the values and goals of social justice, when we do not address structural disparities, the role and purpose of therapy cannot be described as wholly inclusive or beneficial. In regards to the current political and social climate in the United States, there is a re-emergence of particular conservative cultural trends in upholding self-sufficiency, 'gate-watching,' and exclusion of non-mainstream societies, which can undermine our concerns for oppressions, marginalization, inequity, underutilization, inequality of care, and culturally informed practice.

Likewise, we can work as consultants in a preventative capacity regarding efforts that focus on the prevention of mental disorders, better treatment options, and accessibility. Such work also demands continuous reassessment of current social and political climate and consideration of minority and immigrant mental healthcare. In such a way, we can better serve with social responsibility.

In our organizational accountability for American Indians, we are warned that:

> As in every society, the [colonizer] will never work to change the bad situation of the [colonized] . . . The [colonizer] will never free the [colonized] because [they're] comfortable with destroying the [colonized]." (Shalhoub-Kervorkian & Daher-Nashif, 2013, p. 305).

Regarding law enforcement injustice, an AI person said:

> I'd probably have to say I've had some discrimination by cops. Just because they think of me as another Indian. I've had a couple of experiences that I wasn't too happy with about that" (Vancouver focus group). (Ristock et al., 2017, p.778).

Organizational Accountability for Racial Justice

The following statement was made by Gilbert Newman, Vice President of Academic Affairs of Wright Institute, Berkeley, on the listserv of the National Schools and Programs in Professional Psychology (NCSPP). The members of the NCSPP listserv are clinical psychology administrators of the Doctor of Psychology (PsyD) programs. This statement followed soon after the murder of George Floyd by Minneapolis police officers. The email, dated May 28, 2020, was from gnewman@wi.edu to NCSPPDEL@lists.apa.org. This email received positive responses from many PsyD program directors and NCSPP officials, who reported on action steps they were taking within their respective programs to address anti-Black racism.

> The year I became Dean was the year of Trayvon Martin's death at the hands of a

zealous neighborhood watch coordinator. Like the majority of these episodes, Trayvon's killer was acquitted. The Black Lives Matter movement was initiated in response to Trayvon's murder. Opal Tometi, one of the cofounders of Black Lives Matter, decreed "[y]ou have a duty in this moment in history to take action and stand on the side of people who have been oppressed for generations". During the last eight years there have been countless instances of wrongful death of unarmed Black individuals. Eric Garner, Michael Brown, Tante Parker, 12-year-old Tamir Rice, Walter Scott, Ahmaud Arbery, now George Floyd, and there's no end to the names. There is no manner in which I can fully acknowledge the pain my black friends, students, and colleagues suffer knowing that they and their loved ones live in constant fear and/or danger. The rest of us, as heartfelt and caring clinicians to society, as clinical psychologists, we need to support our Black community members and share in this moment the torment these incidents evoke. We must also resolve ourselves to take action.

… I became obsessed (as I am to this day) with trying to understand the holocaust in Europe and in other parts of the world. My family had barely survived anti-semitism. They lived and worked and seemed on the surface to warmly interact with Black and Puerto Rican people in Newark. My mother's high school yearbook had sweet messages inscribed by classmates of color. So, what was their problem? Why express such rancor and why so much fear about Black people and others different from themselves? In college I was introduced to James Baldwin's work, *The Fire Next Time*. I was already becoming an advocate for the rights of the mentally ill and was reading novels, sociology, and psychology to help me understand the nature of oppression. Baldwin's words have stuck with me and have always rung true to me: "I imagine one of the reasons people cling to their hates so stubbornly is because they sense, once hate is gone, they will be forced to deal with pain.

What tangible steps can I take? I want to continue to find ways to call upon our community to show solidarity and to hold each other in our hearts and to voice our support when members of our community are assaulted by events taking place in our nation and throughout the world. I want to enlist my colleagues to think with me about how we can, as a community, take action. I'm very concerned about the political polarization in America and experience racism as a major factor in the divide. In obeisance to Dr. Martin Luther King, Jr., I suggest we take up the advice he provided to psychologists 50 years ago: engage in political action - get out the vote, support candidates of color and others who can support the needs of our Black, Latinx, and other people of color. Support candidates who support women, who support sexual and gender diversity. Apply psychological science and research to persuade voters…May George Floyd and the countless other victims, named and unnamed, throughout centuries of time, rest in peace.

The American Counseling Association (ACA) Anti-Racism Writing Group (June 12, 2020) has been responsible for ACA's statement of solidarity with Black/African Americans. ACA's statement (https://www.counseling.org/news/updates/2020/06/22/aca-anti-racism-statement) follows:

Racism, police brutality, systemic violence, and the dehumanizing forces of oppression, powerlessness, and White supremacy have eroded the very fabric of humanity which ideally binds our society together. Macrolevel systemic racism extends to disparities in institutional policies and procedures in healthcare, education, the judicial system, employment, sports and entertainment, and the brutal violence of law enforcement. These larger societal oppressions lead to inaccessibility to resources and social marginalization, which descend finally to individual racist attitudes, implicit biases, stereotypes, microaggressions, and even death. The ongoing and historical injustices are not acknowledged by those who want to be in power or protect their entitlements. Those who do acknowledge, do so reactively, temporarily, or superficially. There is no course of action for change. Anti-Black racism is often reframed as accidental, an unfortunate incident, or as the criminality of the victim.

Words cannot truly capture our feelings. We are angry, exhausted, grieving, suffering, furious, and in despair. The American Counseling Association mourns because of the pain and murders of George Floyd, Ahmaud Arbery, Breonna Taylor, Tamir Rice, Eric Garner, Sandra Bland, Michael Brown, and countless other Black/African Americans whose identities remain nameless. We stand in solidarity with our Black siblings in denouncing the historical legacy and destruction caused by institutionalized racism and violence against Black people, perpetuated at the hands of law enforcement, the hatred bred of White supremacy, the deafening silence of dehumanizing and complicit inaction to address these systemic ills within our society. As counselors, we listen, we empathize, and agree with protestors that when absolute justice is established, peace will follow. Enough is enough, we cannot continue to watch fellow Black Americans being murdered and the very life force suffocated out of them.

The American Counseling Association is built on enduring values and a mission that promotes: human dignity and diversity, respect, the attainment of a quality of life for all, empowerment, integrity, social justice advocacy, equity, and inclusion. These words become hollow and meaningless for our members and the counseling community when we remain silent and do not promote racial justice. Given the rapidly evolving double pandemic of COVID-19 and the continued exposure of Black people to institutionalized racism, ACA wants to be clear about where we stand and the ongoing actions we will take. As proactive leaders, counselors, mentors, supervisors, scholars, and trainers we will break away from this structure of racism trauma, and the violence born on the necks of Black people.

Our stance is: Black Lives Matter. We have a moral and professional obligation to infiltrate and deconstruct institutions which have historically been designed to benefit White America. These systems must be dismantled in order to level the playing field for Black communities. Allyship is not enough. We strive to create liberated spaces in the fight against White supremacy and the dehumanization of Black people. The burden of transgenerational trauma should not be shouldered by Black Americans even though they have remained resilient. (ACA June 12, 2020)

Additionally, all members must be willing to challenge these systems, but also confront one's own biases, stereotypes, and racial worldview.

Conclusion

All people, including racial, ethnic, LGBTQ+, the poor, and people with disabilities have a right to equitable treatment, allocation of societal resources, and decision-making. Broadly, it has been estimated that American Indian peoples experience rates of psychological distress 1.5 times higher than the general population (ApA, 2010). In 2014, approximately 21% of AI/ANs ages 18 and older reported experiencing some form of mental illness as compared to

17.9% of the general population (APA, 2017). Improving mental health can be particularly difficult when surrounded by negative social contexts that do not allow for practice of positive coping skills.

Psychological professionals can support clients, students, research participants, and consultees in a range of systemic ways that go beyond clinical work, teaching, research, and consultation. These larger contextual roles, for instance, can include our work as advocating for public policies, engaging in public health endeavors, working to promote access and utilization of services in systems of care, and getting funding to affect the well-being of the public at large. Utilizing advocacy's systems perspective creates a socially responsive voice for underserved and under-supported populations. Being involved in public policy strengthens the voice and presence of psychology in the public domain. Specific recommendations for our role in applying research to shape public policy include learning to be strategic, including identifying who the stakeholders and decision-makers are; identifying information gaps that exist and the best way to communicate what needs to be known; evaluating the effectiveness and costs of existing programs and also developing programs to address key public health issues; and developing relationships with policymakers so that progress can be made. Shaping public policy on key issues related to disparity is a complex and multifaceted process that requires our persistence and resilience.

References

Adams, G., Gómez Ordóñez, L., Kurtiş, T., Molina, L. E., & Dobles, I. (2017). Notes on decolonizing psychology: From one special issue to another. *South African Journal of Psychology*, *47*(4), 531-541. https://doi.org/10.1177/0081246317738173

American Psychiatric Association. (2010). *Mental health disparities: American Indians and Alaska Natives [APA Fact Sheet]*. Retrieved from https://www.integration. samhsa.gov/workforce/mental_health_disparities_a merican_indian_and_ alaskan_natives.pdf

American Psychiatric Association. (2017). *Mental health disparities: American Indians and Alaska Natives*. Division of Diversity and Health Equity. Retrieved from http://Downloads/Mental-Health-Facts-for-American-Indian-Alaska-Natives%20(2).pdf

American Psychological Association Center for Workforce Studies. (2017). *Degrees in psychology* [Interactive data tool]. Retrieved from http://www.apa.org/workforce/data-tools/degrees-psychology.aspx

Austin, A. (2013). Native Americans and jobs: The challenge and the promise (Briefing paper 370). Economic Policy Institute.

Bagalman, E., & Heisler, E. J. (2016). Behavioral health among American Indian and Alaska Natives: An overview. Congressional Research Service.

Beals, J., Manson, S. M., Whitesell, N. R., Spicer, P.,
       Novins, D. K., Mitchell, C. M., & AI-SUPERPFP,
       (2005). Prevalence of DSM-IV disorders and
       attendant help-seeking in 2 American Indian
       reservation populations. *Archives of General
       Psychiatry, 62*(1), 99–108.
       https://doi.org/10.1001/archpsyc.62.1.99
Blackwell, D. M. (2010). Sidelines and separate spaces:
       Making education anti-racist for students of
       color. *Race Ethnicity and Education, 13*(4), 473-
       494. https://doi.org/10.1080/13613324.2010.492135
Blake, J. J., Zhou, Q., Kwok, O., & Benz, M. R. (2016).
       Predictors of bullying behavior, victimization, and
       bully-victim risk among high school students with
       disabilities. *Remedial and Special Education, 37*(5),
       285-
       295. https://doi.org/10.1177/0741932516638860
Brockie, T. N., Dana-Sacco, G., Wallen, G. R.,
       Wilcox, H. C., & Campbell, J. C. (2015). The
       relationship of adverse childhood experiences to
       PTSD, depression, poly-drug use and suicide
       attempt in reservation-based Native American
       adolescents and young adults. *American Journal of
       Community Psychology, 55*(3-4), 411-
       421. https://doi.org/10.1007/s10464-015-9721-3
Brondolo, E., Byer, K., Gianaros, P. J., Liu, C., Prather, A.
       A., Thomas, K., & Woods-Giscombé, C. L. (2017).
       Stress and health disparities: Contexts, mechanisms
       and interventions among racial/ethnic minority and
       low socioeconomic status populations. APA.
Brown, L. S. (2018). *Theories of psychotherapy series.
       Feminist therapy (2nd ed.).* American Psychological
       Association. https://doi.org/10.1037/0000092-000

Buchwald, D., Beals, J., & Manson, S. M. (2000). Use of traditional health practices among Native Americans in a primary care setting. *Medical Care, 38*(12), 1191-1199. https://doi.org/10.1097/00005650-200012000-00006

Carter, R. T. (2007). Racism and psychological and emotional injury. *The Counseling Psychologist, 35*(1), 13-105. https://doi.org/10.1177/0011000006292033

Centers for Disease Control and Prevention. (2013). *CDC health disparities and inequalities report* (Supplement No. 62(3)). Retrieved from https://www.cdc.gov/mmwr/pdf/other/su6203.pdf

Comas-Díaz, L., Hall, G. N., & Neville, H. A. (2019). Racial trauma: Theory, research, and healing: Introduction to the special issue. *American Psychologist, 74*(1), 1-5. https://doi.org/10.1037/amp0000442

Cook, E. E., Nickerson, A. B., Werth, J. M., & Allen, K. P. (2016). Service providers' perceptions of and responses to bullying of individuals with disabilities. *Journal of Intellectual Disabilities, 21*(4), 277-296. https://doi.org/10.1177/1744629516650127

Corrigan, P. W., Markowitz, F. E., & Watson, A. C. (2004). Structural levels of mental illness stigma and discrimination. *Schizophrenia Bulletin, 30*(3), 481-491. https://doi.org/10.1093/oxfordjournals.schbul.a007096

David, E. (2013). *Internalized oppression: The psychology of marginalized groups*. Springer Publishing Company.

Diefenbach, M. A., & Leventhal, H. (1996). The common-sense model of illness representation: Theoretical and practical considerations. *Journal of Social Distress and the Homeless, 5*(1), 11-38. https://doi.org/10.1007/bf02090456

Duran, E., Duran, B., Yellow Horse Brave Heart, M., & Yellow Horse-Davis, S. (1998). Healing the American Indian soul wound. In U. Danieleli (Ed.) *International* Handbook of Multigenerational Legacies of Trauma, 341-354. Plenum.

Freire, P. (1972). *Pedagogy of the oppressed.* Penguin.

Garrett, M. T., Awe Agahe Portman, T., Williams, C., Grayshield, L., Torres Rivera, E.,

Parrish, M. (2012). Native American adult lifespan perspectives: Where power moves. In E. Chang E., & C. Downey. (Eds.) (2012), *Handbook of race and development in mental health* (pp. 107-126). Springer.

Garrett, M. T., Garrett, J. T., Torres-Rivera, E., Wilbur, M., & Roberts-Wilbur, J. (2005). Laughing it up: Native American humor as spiritual tradition. *Journal of Multicultural Counseling and Development, 33*(4), 194-204. https://doi.org/10.1002/j.2161-1912.2005.tb00016.x

Gone, J. P., Hartmann, W. E., Pomerville, A., Wendt, D. C., Klem, S. H., & Burrage, R. L. (2019). The impact of historical trauma on health outcomes for Indigenous populations in the USA and Canada: A systematic review. *American Psychologist, 74*(1), 20-35. https://doi.org/10.1037/amp0000338

Gone, J. P., & Trimble, J. E. (2012). American Indian and Alaska native mental health: Diverse perspectives on enduring disparities. *Annual Review of Clinical Psychology, 8*(1), 131-160. https://doi.org/10.1146/annurev-clinpsy-032511-143127

Harpur, P. (2009). Sexism and racism, why not
     ableism? *Alternative Law Journal, 34*(3), 163-
     167. https://doi.org/10.1177/1037969x0903400304

Herzig, B. A., Roysircar, G., Kosyluk, K. A., &
     Corrigan, P. W. (2013). American Muslim college
     students: The impact of religiousness and stigma on
     active coping. *Journal of Muslim Mental
     Health, 7*(1). https://doi.org/10.3998/jmmh.1038160
     7.0007.103

Hollander, A., Bruce, D., Burström, B., & Ekblad, S.
     (2011). Gender-related mental health differences
     between refugees and non-refugee immigrants - a
     cross-sectional register-based study. *BMC Public
     Health, 11*(1). https://doi.org/10.1186/1471-2458-
     11-180

Institute of Medicine (US) Committee on the Health
     Professions Education Summit (2003). In A. C.
     Greiner & E. Knebel (Eds.). *Health professions
     education: A bridge to quality*. National Academies
     Press.

Isaac, K. S., Hay, J. L., & Lubetkin, E. I. (2016).
     Incorporating spirituality in primary care. *Journal
     of Religion and Health, 55*(3), 1065-
     1077. https://doi.org/10.1007/s10943-016-0190-2

Kenney, M. K., & Singh, G. K. (2016). Adverse childhood
     experiences among American Indian/Alaska native
     children: The 2011-2012 national survey of
     children's health. *Scientifica, 2016*, 1-
     14. https://doi.org/10.1155/2016/7424239

Koenig, H. G. (2012). Religion, spirituality, and health:
     The research and clinical implications. *ISRN
     Psychiatry, 2012*, 1-
     33. https://doi.org/10.5402/2012/278730

LaFromboise, T., & Howard-Pitney, B. (1995). The Zuni life skills development curriculum: Description and evaluation of a suicide prevention program. *Journal of Counseling Psychology, 42*(4), 479-486. https://doi.org/10.1037/0022-0167.42.4.479

LaFromboise, T. D., & Malik, S. S. (2016). A culturally informed approach to American Indian/Alaska Native youth suicide prevention. In N. Zane, G. Bernal, & F. T. Leong (Eds.), *Evidence-based psychological practice with ethnic minorities: Culturally informed research and clinical strategies (pp. 223-245)*. https://doi.org/10.1037/14940-011

Lalvani, P., & Bacon, J. K. (2018). Rethinking "We are all special": Anti-ableism curricula in early childhood classrooms. *Young Exceptional Children, 22*(2), 87-100. https://doi.org/10.1177/1096250618810706

Li, H., & Seidman, L. (2010). Engaging Asian American youth and their families in quality mental health services. *Asian Journal of Psychiatry, 3*(4), 169-172. https://doi.org/10.1016/j.ajp.2010.08.008

Logan, E., Blount, S., Mendoza, L., Pittman, C., Ray, R., & Trujillo-Pagan, N. (2013). Double consciousness: Faculty of color teaching students of color about race. *Teaching Race and Anti-Racism in Contemporary America*, 123-139. https://doi.org/10.1007/978-94-007-7101-7_13

Manson, S. M. (2000). Mental health services for American Indians and Alaska Natives: Need, use, and barriers to effective care. *The Canadian Journal of Psychiatry, 45*(7), 617-626. https://doi.org/10.1177/070674370004500703

Martin, D., Yurkovich, E., & Anderson, K. (2016). American Indians' family health concern on a northern plains reservation: "Diabetes runs rampant here". *Public Health Nursing, 33*(1), 73-81. https://doi.org/10.1111/phn.12225

Milburn, N. G., & Lightfoot, M. (2016). Improving participation of families of color in evidence-based interventions: Challenges and lessons learned. In N. Zane, G. Bernal, & F. T. L. Leong (Eds.), *Evidence-based psychological practice with ethnic minorities: Culturally informed research and clinical strategies* (pp. 273-287). APA.

Mitchum, R. (2012). A religious approach to health disparities. *Science Life.* Retrieved from https://sciencelife.uchospitals.edu/2012/06/07/a-religious-approach-to-health-disparities/

Mohatt, N. V., Thompson, A. B., Thai, N. D., & Tebes, J. K. (2014). Historical trauma as public narrative: A conceptual review of how history impacts present-day health. *Social Science & Medicine, 106*, 128-136. https://doi.org/10.1016/j.socscimed.2014.01.04 3

Norris, T., Vines, P. L., & Hoeffel, E. M. (2012). *The American Indian and Alaska Native population: 2010, (2010 Census Briefs No. C2010BR-10; pp. 1–21).* Retrieved from United States Census Bureau website: https://www.census.gov/history/pdf/c2010br-10.pdf

Pachankis, J. E., Hatzenbuehler, M. L., Hickson, F., Weatherburn, P., Berg, R. C., Marcus, U., & Schmidt, A. J. (2015). Hidden from health. *AIDS, 29*(10), 1239-1246. https://doi.org/10.1097/qad.00000000000007 24

Padela, A. I., & Curlin, F. A. (2012). Religion and disparities: Considering the influences of Islam on the health of American Muslims. *Journal of Religion and Health, 52*(4), 1333-1345. https://doi.org/10.1007/s10943-012-9620-y

Parent, M. C., & Silva, K. (2018). Critical consciousness moderates the relationship between transphobia and "bathroom bill" voting. *Journal of Counseling Psychology, 65*(4), 403-412. https://doi.org/10.1037/cou0000270

Pargament, K. I., Smith, B. W., Koenig, H. G., & Perez, L. (1998). Patterns of positive and negative religious coping with major life stressors. *Journal for the Scientific Study of Religion, 37*(4), 710. https://doi.org/10.2307/1388152

Ristock, J., Zoccole, A., Passante, L., & Potskin, J. (2017). Impacts of colonization on Indigenous two-spirit/LGBTQ Canadians' experiences of migration, mobility and relationship violence. *Sexualities, 22*(5-6), 767-784. https://doi.org/10.1177/1363460716681474

Roberts, L., Mann, S., & Montgomery, S. (2015). Depression, a hidden mental health disparity in an Asian Indian immigrant community. *International Journal of Environmental Research and Public Health, 13*(1), 27. https://doi.org/10.3390/ijerph13010027

Roysircar, G. (2008). A response to "Social privilege, social justice, and group counseling: An inquiry": Social privilege: Counselors' competence with Systemically determined inequalities. *The Journal for Specialists in Group Work, 33*(4), 377-384. https://doi.org/10.1080/01933920802424456

Roysircar G. (2013). Disaster counseling: A Haitian family case post January 12, 2010 earthquake. In S. Poyrazili & C. Thompson (Eds.). *International case studies in mental health (pp.155-180)*. Thousand Oaks, CA: SAGE.

Roysircar, G., Colvin, K. F., Afolayan, A. G.,
Thompson, A., & Robertson, T. W. (2017). Haitian
children's resilience and vulnerability assessed with
house–tree–person (HTP)
drawings. *Traumatology*, *23*(1), 68-
81. https://doi.org/10.1037/trm0000090

Roysircar, G., Geisinger, K. F., & Thompson, A. (2019a).
Haitian children's disaster trauma: Validation of
pictorial assessment of resilience and
vulnerability. *Journal of Black Psychology*, *45*(4),
269-
305. https://doi.org/10.1177/0095798419838126

Roysircar, G., Thompson, A., & Geisinger, K. F. (2019b).
Trauma coping of mothers and children among poor
people in Haiti: Mixed methods study of
community-level research. *American
Psychologist*, *74*(9), 1189-
1206. https://doi.org/10.1037/amp0000542

Safran, M. A., Mays, R. A., Huang, L. N., McCuan, R.,
Pham, P. K., Fisher, S. K., McDuffie, K. Y., &
Trachtenberg, A. (2009). Mental health
disparities. *American Journal of Public
Health*, *99*(11), 1962-
1966. https://doi.org/10.2105/ajph.2009.167346

Shalhoub-Kervorkian, N., & Daher-Nashif, S. (2013).
Femicide and colonization. *Violence Against
Women*, *19*(3), 295-
315. https://doi.org/10.1177/1077801213485548

Seward, D. X. (2014). Multicultural course pedagogy:
Experiences of Master's-level students of
color. *Counselor Education and Supervision*, *53*(1),
62-79. https://doi.org/10.1002/j.1556-
6978.2014.00049.x

Smith, S. D., Hall, J. P., & Kurth, N. K. (2020).
     Perspectives on health policy from people with
     disabilities. *Journal of Disability Policy Studies*,
     104420732095667. https://doi.org/10.1177/1044207
     320956679

Speight, S. L. (2007). Internalized racism: One more piece
     of the puzzle. *The Counseling Psychologist, 35*(1),
     126-134.
     https://doi.org/10.1177/0011000006295119

Terrell, F., & Terrell, S. (1984). Race of counselor, client
     sex, cultural mistrust level, and premature
     termination from counseling among Black
     clients. *Journal of Counseling Psychology, 31*(3),
     371-375. https://doi.org/10.1037/0022-
     0167.31.3.371

The White House Office of the Press Secretary (2013,
     December 4). *Remarks by the President on
     economic mobility*. Retrieved from
     https://obamawhitehouse.archives.gov/the-press-
     office/2013/12/04/remarks-president-economic-
     mobility

Tucker, R. P., Wingate, L. R., O'Keefe, V. M.,
     Hollingsworth, D. W., & Cole, A. B. (2015). An
     examination of historical loss thinking frequency
     and rumination on suicide ideation in American
     Indian young adults. *Suicide and Life-Threatening
     Behavior, 46*(2), 213-
     222. https://doi.org/10.1111/sltb.12185

Turner, S. L., & Pope, M. (2009). North America's native
     peoples: A social justice and trauma counseling
     approach. *Journal of Multicultural Counseling and
     Development, 37*(4), 194-
     205. https://doi.org/10.1002/j.2161-
     1912.2009.tb00102.x

Urban Indian Health Institute. (2012). *Addressing depression among American Indians and Alaska Natives: A literature review*. Retrieved from http://www.uihi.org/wp-content/uploads/2012/08/Depression-Environmental-Scan_All-Sections_2012-08-21_ES_FINAL.pdf

van Zomeren, M., Postmes, T., & Spears, R. (2008). Toward an integrative social identity model of collective action: A quantitative research synthesis of three socio-psychological perspectives. *Psychological Bulletin, 134*(4), 504-535. https://doi.org/10.1037/0033-2909.134.4.504

Ward, E. C. (2002). *Cultural competence, cultural mistrust, working alliance and racial ethnic minority clients' experience of counseling: A mixed method study*. University of Wisconsin-Madison.

Chapter 4: Transnationalism: A Case Study of a Pakistani Muslim Woman

Globalization, international geopolitics, and growth in digital technologies have drawn the world into a complex network of social, business, and military engagements, ensuring that intersectional identities are experienced multi-dimensionally and globally. Concurrent with this, a resulting dynamic interaction of local, national, and cross-national psychologies has enhanced our understanding of indigenous, culture-specific, shared, and unique aspects of behavior and identity development. Multilateral and horizontal dialogues among psychology professionals working collaboratively on transnational projects allow for the exploration of questions about what it means to be human across universal, local, indigenous, communal, and individualistic considerations, better allowing psychology to be practiced broadly in global contexts. In addition, psychologists, as key constituents in the establishment of social justice, strive more readily to develop coalition-building with practitioners across nationalities to address oppression, disempowerment, and trauma.

It is notable that now one traumatic event in one city in one part of the world, such as episodes of terrorism experienced in the recent past in Mumbai, London, Paris, Pittsburg, Sri Lanka, and Christchurch, can reverberate globally, influencing responses across the countries of the world. As psychologists, even though we may be acting locally, we can still find ourselves wrestling with actions and responses to events taking place globally. As a result, there is a greater requirement that we understand human conditions in a broad, global context. As psychologists we now theorize about universal conditions of trauma, resilience, oppression, empowerment, and human rights and dignity, while also operationalizing and seeking to address culture-specific manifestations of these universal experiences (Roysircar et al., 2021b). The following case illustration is used to help demonstrate the ways in which an understanding of transnationalism can inform clinical practice, teaching, research, and consultation.

Case Illustration—Fatima

Case is adapted from the novel, Saffron Dreams (2009), written by Shaila Abdullah and published by Modern History Press.

Fatima is a 45-year-old, Muslim woman who was born in Karachi, Pakistan. She was raised by her father, Sultan, and lived with her siblings Mumtaz and Salim. Her mother, Ameena, was not emotionally present during her upbringing; she was absent from her marriage, with a history of extramarital affairs. While such relationships are against the law in Pakistan, the family's high social status meant that no legal action was ever brought against them for Ameena's choices and actions. When considering her relationship to her mother, Fatima notably recalled at least one occasion when her mother expressed disdain for her, stating her regret for having Fatima as a child. Fatima has remained distant from her mother but has maintained good relationships with all other members of her family.

Fatima met her husband, Abdul, through a matchmaker hired by her father. Abdul was an aspiring writer. Following their marriage, Fatima and Abdul relocated to New York City (NYC), where Abdul worked in a retail store in the World Trade Center while pursuing his writing career. After only three years of marriage, Abdul was killed in the attacks on the World Trade Center in September 2001. At that time, Fatima was several months pregnant with their first child. Importantly, Fatima was not identified as a beneficiary of the 9/11 widows' compensation; as a result, she and her soon-to-be-born child were left financially distressed following her husband's death.

Fatima further reported that she found living in NYC as a Muslim woman post-9/11 to be difficult. She shared that on one occasion she was attacked in a subway station at knifepoint by a group of teenage boys who made it clear that her identity as a Muslim was their motive for attacking her. After enduring many stares, comments, and even physical threats, Fatima made the choice to no longer wear her *hijab* (head covering), to ensure greater safety and to draw less attention to herself. In therapy Fatima reported feeling specifically guilty about this decision. To discontinue wearing the hijab symbolized a loss of both her Muslim identity and the connection to her late husband, who was traditional in his expectations. She also reported feelings of survivor guilt, helplessness, displacement, and of being a victim herself of the 9/11 attacks.

Fatima's parents came to the United States on a visitor's visa, following her husband's death. Their plan was to help care for her. Fatima shared that her in-laws were a tremendous support system for her at that time, and notably, on her mother-in-law's insistence, Fatima decided to complete Abdul's unfinished novel. As Fatima prepared for the birth of the child, it became known that he would be born with disabilities. As a result of this increased stress, Fatima decided to move to Houston to be closer to an uncle and to relocate away from the post 9/11 environment of NYC. Her parents returned to Pakistan on the expiration of their visitor's visa.

Fatima's son, Faizal, was born in Houston. He was identified over time as having several significant disabilities, including deafness, an inability to speak, and partial blindness. During their multiple visits to the hospital for Faizal's care, Fatima came to meet Hussain, a Pakistani health professional with whom she developed a growing, close relationship.

In therapy, Fatima shared that she had many reservations about entering into a relationship with a man who was not her husband. She further reported that while she and Hussain reached a point of engaging in sexual activity, her feelings about the situation remained complicated and negative. This inability to feel comfortable with intimacy with Hussain, as well as differences of opinion they had about other areas of daily life, including parenting, prompted the relationship to end.

Fatima has settled into life in Houston, where she works part-time for a non-profit magazine and is a single parent. She is also enrolled in a Master of Fine Arts (MFA) creative writing program that is largely online. Fatima continues to seek ways to build her life forward, while also honoring the memory of her husband, and parenting their child. Her feelings about being a Muslim woman in the U.S. remain complicated and she still experiences discomfort apart from her home country.

Personal Reflection Questions

- What feelings do you notice coming up as you read about Fatima? How might these feelings support your understanding of Fatima versus how might your feelings be an interpretation of how you imagine Fatima herself feels?
- What immediate thoughts are coming to mind? Do you notice yourself asking questions that are based in trying to determine a diagnosis or treatment? What would it be like to focus on understanding Fatima's story and experiences?

Discussion Questions Related to Fatima

- What are the intersectional identities Fatima presents in therapy?

- How would you work with Fatima to address this intersectionality?
- How would you address the multiple losses Fatima has faced in her life (i.e., the loss of her own mother due to her inattention, the loss of her husband, the loss of feeling able to wear the *hijab*, the loss of her native country)?
- What are the parenting issues Fatima might face in raising her son?
- How might you partner with Fatima to support her role as a parent whose son has various disabilities?
- Fatima has experienced intense discrimination related to being a Muslim woman. In therapy, how can you support Fatima as a Muslim woman living in the U.S.?

Literature Review

While the United States remains identified as a major corporate and military power with significant influence on the world's economic, social, and political activities, globalization and international immigration that are active across the main Western nations of the world have meant that imbalances and inequities are significant. This has an impact on many aspects of life for individuals with whom we as psychologists interact. Furthermore, the engagement of the United States in many varied struggles that have developed or are building across the world has meant that, in tandem with our 24/7 immediate access to global information, traumas and discord are shared rapidly. For immigrant communities within the United States, information about home, as well as sharing of challenges within their new U.S. environments with their peers and families, sometimes with limited contextual understanding, lead to an increased experience of vulnerability and uncertainty across settings.

The past decades' conflicts and wars have led to the development of negative perceptions in many American soldiers and veterans, as well as U.S. citizens that are simultaneous with shared deeply biased views of the varied societies outside the U.S, where conflicts have been fought. In tandem, residents from the countries experiencing wars and strife, who have immigrated to the U.S., have experienced substantial episodes of disrespect and even violence. Fatima's experience of acts of hatred in public places as discussed in the case above provides further evidence of the level of Islamophobia many Muslim immigrants and citizens of the U.S. have had to deal with. With the current changes in travel and immigration policy in the United States that have affected specific Islamic countries in particular, denigration and even trauma have been inflicted.

In working with immigrant communities, it is important to address possible isolation and fear our client's experience. Many who have immigrated to the U.S. are struggling with what it means to live apart from their home culture and familiar support system, specifically when they first are settling into their second country. Efforts to ensure greater stability can involve helping clients build more contacts and supports through potential groups and organizations; this can be a useful therapeutic strategy (Cook-Masaud & Wiggins, 2011). But as the case of Fatima shows, it is also important to explore, as possible, how changes in cultural expectations and traditions affect their sense of both who they are across time and how they can gain some degree of stability regarding their self-identity. Addressing the personal understanding a client presents regarding gender roles, marriage, and how the death of a spouse may affect those components of identity is also an important goal. As clinicians we may find a need to advocate for connections with legal and advocacy supports for our clients.

Transnationalism

Transnationalism offers an important set of resources for theorizing culture-specific experiences of psychological suffering and distress. Its key feature is the warning against imposing the frames of reference and moral visions of Western high-income countries, which is called the Minority World, on the Majority World (Arnett, 2008). The terms Minority World/Majority World replace older designations like First World/Third World and developed/ developing countries, which are seen as problematic (Arnett, 2008). The term Minority World underscores the fact that Western high-income countries account for less than 15% of the world's population (Arnett, 2008). By using the term Majority World, psychologists avoid the presumption of a universal trajectory of progress with Western high-income countries at the pinnacle.

Some transnational feminists have advised American feminist practitioners and researchers from viewing themselves as providers of modern or rational knowledge to women in international settings, which was the civilizing mission of the colonial era (Collins et al., 2019). When Minority World psychologists cross national borders, they need to be attuned to the particularities of localities they serve—the culturally-embedded goals, moral visions, and lifeways that shape gendered experiences (Collins et al., 2019). Similarly, when psychologists cross national borders (or engage in psychotherapy/counseling with border-crossing clients), it is crucial that they bring transnational, decolonial, and critical social justice perspectives to their work (Roysircar et al., 2019a, 2021b).

In U.S. psychology, concepts of self and personhood form the basis for norms of acceptable behavior, judgments about psychological disorder and well-being, approaches to intimate relationships, and moral visions (Ginter et al., 2018). The focus on the individual self confers a high value on liberty, equality, autonomy, privacy, choice, self-fulfillment, and individual expression. Becoming mature is taken to mean becoming self-defining, that is, to be able to step outside of binds and social constraints and to craft who one will be (Ginter et al., 2018). This view of maturity has shaped psychologists' theories of child development, especially adolescent development.

People in the Majority World, however, may have many selves with fluid and permeable boundaries that are inextricably embedded in kin relations. Many live in rural or semi-rural communities, often sharing a household or compound with multiple generations of extended family members. They are related through consanguineal ties, marriage, and clanship. Their relationships likely extend back through many generations, and people anticipate that their intergenerational relationships will extend into the future as well. These relationships are not necessarily harmonious. They may be fractured by animosities, betrayals, grudges, sexism, heterosexism, power hierarchies, alcoholism, infidelity, and abuse. Nonetheless, in such social settings, personhood and self are experienced in ways that are not in keeping with the individualist ethos of the Minority World. Cultural models of well-being also differ from those put forward in American psychologies (Roysircar et al., 2019a). Conceptions of maturity differ as well; therefore, the goals and practices of childrearing often do not correspond to those prescribed by Minority World psychologists. However, different models of personhood also exist within multicultural U.S. society, which may shift across the life course and in response to cultural, economic, and societal contingencies (Markus & Kitayama, 2003).

Studies of everyday lives in Haiti point out the high value placed on relationality, mutuality, and reciprocity (Roysircar, 2013; Roysircar et al., 2019 a, b, 2021b). Despite their deep involvements in Haiti, Roysircar and her fellow clinicians and researchers acknowledge that they remain outsiders to the Haitian communities they serve. U.S. practitioners are endowed with considerably more power and privilege than their clients and research participants because of their class backgrounds, professional status, and English language fluency. These practitioners recognize that heir positionalities likely impose limits on their ability to comprehend fully the meanings that Haitians put forward (Roysircar et al., 2021b).

There are variations in experiences of transnationalism among people who relocate across the globe. For example, "parachute kids" (i.e., children and adolescents who arrive in the United States without their parents or primary caregivers) are a growing community in U.S. and Canadian schools (Ying, 2001). Often not well prepared for their international journey and the subsequent transition to their new lives, parachute kids may face academic and cultural pressures with little support from adults. The increase in pressure along with a potential lack of support and isolation may place parachute kids at risk for depression, problems with communication, peer pressure, substance use and dependence, gang recruitment, and interpersonal issues with family members (Lee & Friedlander, 2014). Similarly, "Third Culture Kids" (TCKs) refers to young people who are raised in countries other than their primary country of residence. TCKs who return to their birth/first culture may face challenges secondary to cultural marginalization, social isolation, relationship difficulties, low self-esteem, and work or school performance problems, as well as feeling like an outsider when returning to their culture of origin (Pollock & Van Reken, 2009; Zilber, 2009). Parachute kids and TCKs are different from children of immigrants who live with their families and are affiliated with cultural organizations and immigrant communities (Roysircar et al., 2021a).

Systems must be decolonized for actual societal transformation (Carolissen et al., 2017). Most cultures have "politics of exclusion," in which at least one cultural group is systemically designed to maintain power (Shalhoub-Kervorkian & Daher-Nashif, 2013). Legal systems, for example, have been shaped by colonialism, and they support a colonial agenda even when it differs from the popular opinion. Shalhoub-Kervorkian and Daher-Nashif (2013) conducted a qualitative study of a Palestinian community of women living in Israel who are victimized by femicide. Even when men in the community largely also rejected the killing of local women, the legal support of "honor killings" dissuaded people from reporting.

> There are girls who do not go to the police because they see that the police don't do anything. They see killers who were taken to jail as killers and were released after less than 12 years and walking in the street like heroes . . . The girls don't trust the police any more . . . ." (Shalhoub-Kervorkian & Daher-Nashif, 2013, p. 307).

Acculturation Issues

Acculturation is a culture-learning process. It is related to the environmental structures that support and guide development and is sensitive to changes in family relations, health status, addictions and mental health, and other variables often of strong interest to us as psychologists (Chun et al., 2003). More specifically, acculturation is a significant variable when assessing attitudes towards therapy, help-seeking behaviors, and utilization of help resources by immigrant groups (e.g., Asian immigrants, Frey & Roysircar, 2006). Furthermore, across immigrant groups, when working with less acculturated clients, we benefit from collaboration with the community, taking on the role of consultant, advisor, advocate, and facilitator to connect clients to indigenous support systems and indigenous healing systems as these may be helpful (Atkinson et al., 1993). It is also useful to recognize that some immigrant groups may have trouble relating to services provided from a Western framework (Omizo et al., 2008; Roland, 2006; Roysircar et al., 2021a).

Internet and Social Networks

Increased possibilities of communicating across the globe through the internet and social networking have allowed people to build connections and attachments with others globally. We now have the ability to associate with a wider range of peers and engage in educational and work opportunities that are international in scope. With this increased connectivity, national and cultural boundaries are able to be bypassed and reconfigured.

Nonetheless, our increased U.S. engagement with global diversity and its opportunity for expanding our capacity for greater intimacy with others of differing beliefs and cultural norms have led some individuals to become more fearful and anxious about "the other," contributing to increased xenophobia and negative attitudes regarding globalization and immigration. Referring back to our case, it may prove useful to foster greater connections for Fatima via social media and web-based applications to assist in decreasing her sense of isolation. Support networks for parents of children with disabilities, or connections with the variety of mental health apps that offer online access to programs to address mental health conditions including depression and anxiety (https://www.youtube.com/c/thepsychshow) may prove helpful for her. Additionally, she may find that use of such online therapy sites as Talkspace, which provide "private and secure" mental health connections without requiring an office visit can be helpful when dealing with a crisis.

Considerations for Clinical Practice

Culture provides the contexts in which personality and mental disorders can be understood (Roysircar et al., 2021a). When working with such needs as suicide prevention, family therapy for intergenerational conflicts, and stress management, several culturally based interventions have been shown to be effective. These interventions include the incorporation of Créole prayers within sessions with the help of translators and Catholic priests for Haitian clients (Roysircar, 2013); the application of spiritual metaphors and symbolism when conducting therapy with Dominican immigrants (Roysircar & Pignatiello, 2015); and the imagining of the flora and fauna of one's heritage culture in imagery and relaxation exercises (La Roche, 2006).

Returning to the case of Fatima, we utilize Ibrahim and Dykeman's (2011) review of specific considerations when working with Muslim clients who live in the United States. We as therapists benefit significantly from an understanding of the range of Islamic practices that exist, and how differences across Muslim cultures intersect with those of the U.S. Some clients may struggle with the balance between their commitment to Islamic ideals and the difficulties they may find remaining deeply engaged with their faith in their U.S. home environment. The authors note that it is important to attend to views about gender that Muslim clients may hold, that make working with a therapist of the opposite sex uncomfortable, as more traditional Muslims often limit interactions with the opposite sex outside of their immediate family (Ibrahim & Dykeman, 2011).

Cook-Masaud and Wiggins (2011) have offered considerations regarding the stress some Muslim women experience given differences in women's roles in the United States versus their Islamic culture. Referring back to our case, Fatima's adherence to traditional customs as a widow and mother are important considerations in treatment and can be contrasted with her perception of her mother's choices regarding her marriage and parenting role. Adherence to a more traditional model may be a response to the childhood attachment and trauma experiences Fatima had faced.

Cook-Masaud and Wiggins (2011) have reminded us that Muslims come to the U.S. for a variety of reasons that may need to be explored within treatment. Similarly, their process of adaptation to life in the U.S. and how cultural differences they have experienced may bring about conflicts and challenges may be important topics of therapy. Adapting to a life in a highly individualistic environment from one that has been collectivist can bring about several struggles that we may need to address when working with Muslim clients (Cook-Masaud & Wiggins, 2011).

A way to build rapport with an immigrant Muslim client is to have them share their relocation story and what that change has been like for them. Being collectivistic, Muslims may be uncomfortable with sharing personal details about themselves and their families, in an effort to avoid bringing shame to their family. It may also be challenging for a Muslim client to be open about anything that may be viewed as a fault or shortcoming of their own or others. This tendency may impede the therapeutic process (Hodge & Nadir, 2008). Muslim clients may also take on a passive role and let you the therapist take control based on their socialization in more hierarchical relational dynamics (Cook-Masaud & Wiggins, 2011).

It is common for Muslims to view mental illness and emotional difficulties as issues of faith and involving their network of support. Islam is a holistically based religion, so Muslims tend to view health within a framework of the mind, body, and soul being connected, and they are more likely to experience emotional difficulties in a physical, somatic way (Cook-Masaud & Wiggins, 2011). Thus, Muslims may seek help from medical professionals as a first option, leading to the need for a warm handoff by their physician as a means to establish sufficient rapport with the mental health provider. Acknowledging client-therapist cultural differences at the start of therapy is helpful when working with Muslim clients, allowing open ongoing conversation (Cook-Masaud & Wiggins, 2011).

Muslim individuals often place importance on actions and behaviors in accordance with the *Qur'an*. Muslims also believe in fatality and that challenges may be the will of God, which can have causal effects on human suffering and illness. Beshai et al. (2013) have highlighted the nuanced relationship between the will of God and the free will of individuals that exists for many Muslims, so as not to disregard a person's autonomy.

When considering Fatima's traumatic experiences, specifically being a 9/11 widow and the birth of a child with severe medical disabilities, her approach to making sense of these experiences can be understood from within a faith-based deterministic orientation, while her endurance can be seen as individually motivated moral behaviors. These distinctions of common practices and beliefs in the Muslim tradition (God's will and individual forbearance) are essential to consider when working with Muslim clients, regardless of the theoretical approach of therapy. Hodge and Nadir (2008) stress several core Muslim ideals that are a basis of identity, including sense of community and consensus, interdependency, and a self situated within one's culture, religion, and family. Community often refers to the individual's family or other people identifying as Muslims and practicing Islam. However, there is diversity present to the extent to which individuals adapt more to the U.S. culture or maintain a strong sense of traditional Islamic standards, and such a distinction needs consideration when doing therapy with Muslim immigrant clients.

Considerations for Teaching and Training

We encourage teaching and training to reflect current trends towards globalization. For the mental health profession, this means looking beyond the borders of the United States to consider international perspectives and experiences. Part of this looking outward involves thinking about psychology as practiced in other countries and not just within the United States. A transnational perspective can be brought into the curriculum in many ways.

Case analysis is one such strategy. Case analysis, similar to the case illustrations presented throughout this book, allows students to understand the complexities of different types of international experiences and related intersectional identities. Similarly, case analysis, as with the case of Fatima, helps students grapple with and understand specific issues connected with an immigration experience and immigration status.

Awareness of legal terms (green card, naturalized citizen, visitor's visa) connected with immigration status, and their implications for clients, is another important area of learning. For instance, being able to distinguish between voluntary immigration, forced migration, refugees, unaccompanied minors, asylum seekers, undocumented immigrants and DACA are important (Hodge and Nadir, 2008). Further, incorporating current policies and political events and their impact on potential clients is another curriculum strategy. Situations such as migrant family separations at the U.S.–Mexico border, the trade war between the United States and China, and U.S.-China political tensions over the spread of COVID-19 pandemic are but a few of these global situations. Incorporating a dialogue about our clients' global contexts involves understanding more about country crises they may have experienced.

Issues related to human rights such as torture are not generally addressed in graduate programs (http://www.nepsy.com/articles/leading-stories/graduate-programs-fail-to-address-torture-issue). Similarly, trainees need to take on the ethical issues of psychologists working in potentially coercive settings, such as places of incarceration. Conversations about fairness and justice need to commence during training and supervision. Students of color have noted "difficulty navigating an institutional culture that expects them to diversify the profession, yet is unwilling to adapt to their needs and experiences" (Delgado-Romero et al., 2018, p. 349). Curtis-Boles and Bourg (2010) noted that students of color in their study felt they had gained new knowledge about themselves and other cultural groups through participation in a multicultural counseling course but also acknowledged that the class was emotionally painful and taxing. Taking the time within the course to speak explicitly to this process, working to create a learning environment where students are to take risks and are open to feedback and discussing strategies to mitigate harm is essential. Haskins et al. (2015) noted that by not including information for students of color on how to navigate working with White/White American clients, including how to deal with microaggressions that may occur from client to therapist, an important opportunity is missed to build skills for students of color. As our field continues to diversify, it will be important for educators to move away from the tendency to center the training needs of majority identity students and focus on centering the margins to build courses that do not repeat a marginalization process. Attention to multicultural competence as an aspirational goal is critical for all trainees, researchers, clinicians, and educators.

Students and trainees can also learn about psychology from a transcultural perspective through international service learning and research experience. We encourage students to engage in these programs that provide students with a cultural immersion experience. Students can learn about research through participation in a faculty member's transnational research project or through their own investigation (Roysircar et al., 2017, 2019a, b, 2020b). Students can learn about psychology perspectives that reflect current affairs in the country where they are engaged in service learning. Research has found that engaging in international service learning leads to emotional experiences that not only further academic learning, but also promote understanding about humanness that bind all people, as well as their personal growth (Roysircar et al., 2020b).

International Students

Education has proven an important context where a significant consideration of cultural identities and what they represent within the United States is required. In the 2015-2016 academic year, over one million international students attended colleges and universities in the United States, with Chinese and Indians being the largest international student groups (Open Doors, 2016). International students from 200 countries contributed many billions of dollars to the U.S. economy and supported many thousands of jobs (NAFSA: Association of International Educators, 2016). Similarly, an estimated 10% of American undergraduates are pursuing studies abroad for academic credit (Open Doors, 2016). However, changes in worldwide response to the current U.S. climate for foreign nationals has likely reduced the number of international students in this country's higher education. Enrollments of international students reportedly fell by 6.6% within the 2017-18 academic year when compared to the year before; this marked the second straight year of declines in new enrollments (Open Doors, 2018).

In their review of the literature on Chinese students who come to study in the U.S., Lértora et al. (2017) identified major stressors such as culture shock (e.g., stress prior to arrival to the United States, boredom with small town life of some campuses, language barriers, being away from family), transition shock (e.g., "a state of loss and disorientation precipitated by a change in one's familiar environment that requires adjustment"; Bennett, 1998, p. 216), and acculturative stress (e.g., stress from adjusting to a new culture; Berry, 1997). Other challenges are the complex process of obtaining a student visa and the high cost of higher education in the U.S. (Stringer, 2015). Visas and educational costs are compounded by rules that might limit an international student to only being able to work a certain number of hours per week within one's institution of learning (Stringer, 2015). International students seeking practice experiences will be excluded from federal training sites like VA hospitals because they are not U.S. citizens (Stringer, 2015).

Racial attitudes against immigration in the current political national climate can deter students from reaching new higher education goals as well. It is believed important to identify allies for international students. This can include both classmates and faculty, as well as individuals from among the broader circle of individuals that international students interact with regularly. Faculty and staff having mentoring relationships with international students facilitate their adaptation, career development, and feelings of safety; it allows for the regular guidance and skill building that accompany increased self-efficacy and assertiveness necessary to build one's goals and bring them to reality.

On a more community level, graduate and undergraduate programs can host events that support international students and provide an opportunity to meet peers. Event programming can be responsive to the needs of international students. In other supportive measures, programming can be implemented for international students during times that campuses tend to close such as for holidays and winter breaks. For international students unable to return home during these times, this can be an isolating experience. Programming such as connecting with faculty during these breaks and having social events can aim to lessen the potential isolation that might result.

Academic expectation is another area of potential stress. International students may struggle with English as a second language. This might lead to feeling insecure about sharing in class (which has the potential to lead to a lower grade if class participation is part of the grade) and/or struggling with writing assignments. As faculty and supervisors, we can be sensitive to these issues and encourage a classroom that reflects a safe environment. On an institutional level, institutions can offer student writing services.

Considerations for Research

Research is needed on the nature and status of the mental health professions in different countries. This knowledge is important as it can help us examine the possibility of a "global helping paradigm" that connects mental health services worldwide (Suzuki et al., 2019). Research about the status of mental health services in different countries can help us think about what a global helping paradigm looks like. A starting point is to examine the global burden of disease (GBD), meaning the status of mental health issues worldwide. From there we can consider areas of inquiry that are needed given limitations in currently available data, and how these can connect to support the development of a global helping paradigm.

In identifying gaps in services, one area is to examine how nations can learn from one another. What are the strategies that different nations are engaging in to be responsive to the mental health needs of diverse communities? How might these strategies apply to other nations? Answers to these questions lead to exploring how to leverage these resources. Are there ways in which nations can scale up interventions to share with one another? Are there innovative technologies that can be researched and shared with other nations? These are all research questions that can further seek to build a global helping paradigm.

Considerations for Consultation

Consultation can address mental health disparities domestically and internationally. Domestically, we as psychologists can consult with organizations about how to change policies and practices so that mental health services are more accessible. This might involve working with organizations to decrease wait times to be seen, managing health insurance policies, providing services at convenient hours, making treatment accessible (i.e., coming to the client's home) as needed, and providing services that reflect the cultures and languages of the communities they are serving.

Internationally, mental health resources are not equitably distributed across nations. Resource constrained low and lower-middle income countries often lack a mental health infrastructure (WHO, 2009). This is particularly true when we consider supports for children and adolescents. Building mental health capacity in low and lower-middle income countries is a critical area of consultation for the 21st century.

Conclusion

As our world is increasingly global, our world as helping professionals also expands. While we face significant global challenges at this point in the 21st century, innovations in transportation, technology, social networks, and education provide opportunities for us to bridge the domestic and international divide. Whether working with international students in classrooms situated in the U.S., engaging in transnational mental health practice, conducting transnational research, or supervising students involved in international service learning or study abroad programs, the scope and focus of our roles create multitudinous bridges that intersect between and among nations.

References

Arnett, J. J. (2008). The neglected 95%: Why American psychology needs to become less American. *American Psychologist, 63*(7), 602-614. https://doi.org/10.1037/0003-066x.63.7.602

Atkinson, D. R., Thompson, C. E., & Grant, S. K. (1993). A three-dimensional model for counseling racial/Ethnic minorities. *The Counseling Psychologist, 21*(2), 257-277. https://doi.org/10.1177/0011000093212010

Bennett, Milton, J. (1998). Intercultural communication: A current perspective. In Milton J. Bennett (Ed.). *Basic concepts of intercultural communication: Selected readings*. Intercultural Press.

Berry, J. W. (1997). Immigration, acculturation, and adaptation. *Applied Psychology: An International Review, 46*(1), 5–34. https://doi.org/10.1080/026999497378467

Carolissen, R., Canham, H., Fourie, E., Graham, T., Segalo, P., & Bowman, B. (2017). Epistemological resistance towards diversality: Teaching community psychology as a decolonial project. *South African Journal of Psychology, 47*(4), 495-505. https://doi.org/10.1177/0081246317739203

Chun, K. M., Balls Organista, P., & Marín, G. (Eds.). (2003). *Acculturation: Advances in theory, measurement, and applied research*. APA.

Collins, L. H., Machizawa, S., & Rice, J. K. (Eds.) (2019). Transnational psychology of women: Expanding international and intersectional approaches. APA Books.

Cook-Masaud, C., & Wiggins, M. I. (2011). Counseling Muslim women: Navigating cultural and religious challenges. *Counseling and Values, 55*(2), 247-256. https://doi.org/10.1002/j.2161-007x.2011.tb00035.x

Curtis-Boles, H., & Bourg, E. (2010). Experiences of students of color in a graduate-level diversity course. *Training and Education in Professional Psychology, 4*(3), 204-212. https://doi.org/10.1037/a0017985

Delgado-Romero, E. A., De Los Santos, J., Raman, V. S., Merrifield, J. N., Vazquez, M. S., Monroig, M. M., Bautista, E. C., & Durán, M. Y. (2018). Caught in the middle: Spanish-speaking bilingual mental health counselors as language brokers. *Journal of Mental Health Counseling, 40*(4), 341-352. https://doi.org/10.17744/mehc.40.4.06

Frey, L. L., & Roysircar, G. (2006). South Asian and east Asian international students' perceived prejudice, acculturation, and frequency of help resource utilization. *Journal of Multicultural Counseling and Development, 34*(4), 208-222. https://doi.org/10.1002/j.2161-1912.2006.tb00040.x

Ginter, E. J., Roysircar, G., & Gerstein, L. H. (2018). *Theories and applications of counseling and psychotherapy: Relevance across cultures and settings*. SAGE Publications.

Haskins, N. H., Phelps, R. E., & Crowell, C. (2015). Critically examining Black students' preparation to counsel white clients. *The Journal of Counselor Preparation and Supervision*. https://doi.org/10.7729/73.1077

Hodge, D. R., & Nadir, A. (2008). Moving toward culturally competent practice with Muslims: Modifying cognitive therapy with Islamic tenets. *Social Work, 53*(1), 31-41. https://doi.org/10.1093/sw/53.1.31

Ibrahim, F. A., & Dykeman, C. (2011). Counseling Muslim Americans: Cultural and spiritual assessments. *Journal of Counseling & Development, 89*(4), 387-396. https://doi.org/10.1002/j.1556-6676.2011.tb02835.x

La Roche, M. J. (2013). *Cultural psychotherapy: Theory, methods, and practice*. SAGE Publications.

Lee, H., & Friedlander, M. L. (2014). Predicting depressive symptoms from acculturative family distancing: A study of Taiwanese parachute kids in adulthood. *Cultural Diversity and Ethnic Minority Psychology, 20*(3), 458-462. https://doi.org/10.1037/a0036524

Lértora, I.M., Sullivan, J.M., & Croffie, A. L. (2017). *They are here, now what do we do? Recommendations for supporting international student transitions*. American Counseling Association. https://www.counseling.org/knowledge-center/vistas/by-subject2/vistas-career/docs/default-source/vistas/supporting-international-student-transitions

Markus, H. R., & Kitayama, S. (2003). A collective fear of the collective: implications of selves and theories of selves. In A. W. Kruglanski & E. T. Higgins (Eds.), *Social psychology: A General Reader*. Psychology Press.

NAFSA: National Association of International Educators
(2016). Retrieved from
https://www.nafsa.org/professional-
resources/research-and-trends/nafsa-research-
connections

Omizo, M. M., Kim, B. S., & Abel, N. R. (2008). Asian
and European American cultural values, bicultural
competence, and attitudes toward seeking
professional psychological help among Asian
American adolescents. *Journal of Multicultural
Counseling and Development, 36*(1), 15-
28. https://doi.org/10.1002/j.2161-
1912.2008.tb00066.x

Open Doors (2016). *Annual Open Doors report.*
https://www.insidehighered.com/news/2016/11/14/a
nnual-open-doors-report-documents-continued-
growth-international-students-us-and-us

Open Doors, (2018). Multiple factors contribute to shifts in
student enrollment. https://www.iie.org/Why-
IIE/Events/2018/11/2018-Open-Doors-Press-
Briefing-Washington-DC

Pollock D. C. & Van Reken, R. E. (2009). *Third Culture
Kids: Growing up among worlds* (Revised edition).
Nicholas Brealey Publishing.

Roland, A. (2006). Across civilizations: Psychoanalytic
therapy with asians and Asian
Americans. *Psychotherapy: Theory, Research,
Practice, Training, 43*(4), 454-
463. https://doi.org/10.1037/0033-3204.43.4.454

Roysircar G. (2013). Disaster counseling: A Haitian family
case post January 12, 2010 earthquake. In S.
Poyrazili & C. Thompson (Eds.). *International case
studies in mental health (pp.155-180).* SAGE
Publications.

Roysircar, G., Geisinger, K. F., & Thompson, A. (2019b). Haitian children's disaster trauma: Validation of pictorial assessment of resilience and vulnerability. *Journal of Black Psychology, 45*(4), 269-305. https://doi.org/10.1177/0095798419838126

Roysircar, G., Masseratagah, T., Tran, Q., Niezvestnaya, M., & Thompson, A. (2021a, in press). Asian Indian immigrant youth anxiety: A model minority's generational differences. *Journal of Multicultural Counseling and Development.*

Roysircar, G., & Pignatiello, V. (2015). Counseling and psychotherapy in the USA: The story of Rolando. In R. Moodley, M. Sookoor, U. Gielen, & R. Wu (Eds.), *Therapy without borders: International and cross-cultural case studies handbook (pp. 165-172)*. ACA.

Roysircar, G., Suzuki, L., & Primavera, A, (2021b, submitted). Social justice and transnational counseling competence in Haiti: Qualitative analyses of clinicians' self-reflections. *International Perspectives in Psychology: Research, Practice, and Consultation.*

Roysircar, G., Thompson, A., & Geisinger, K. F. (2019b). Trauma coping of mothers and children among poor people in Haiti: Mixed methods study of community-level research. *American Psychologist, 74*(9), 1189-1206. https://doi.org/10.1037/amp0000542

Shalhoub-Kervorkian, N., & Daher-Nashif, S. (2013). Femicide and colonization. *Violence Against Women, 19*(3), 295-315. https://doi.org/10.1177/1077801213485548

Stringer, H. (2015). Students from abroad: Graduate students from other countries face unique challenges in the United States. https://www.apa.org. https://www.apa.org/gradpsyc h/2015/09/international-students

Suzuki, L. A., O'Shaughnessy, T. A., Roysircar, G., Ponterotto, J. G., & Carter, R. T. (2019). Counseling psychology and the amelioration of oppression: Translating our knowledge into action. *The Counseling Psychologist, 47*(6), 826-872. https://doi.org/10.1177/0011000019888763

World Health Organization (2009). *Strengthening the health sector response to adolescent health and development*. WHO. http://www.who.int/child_adolescent_health/docum ents/cah_adh_flyer_2010/en/index.html

Ying, Y. W. (2001). Migration and cultural orientation: An empirical test of the psychoanalytic theory in Chinese Americans. Journal of Applied Psychoanalytic Studies, 3, 409 – 430. doi:10.1023/A:1012513306348

Zilber, E. (2009). Third culture kids: The children of educators in international schools. John Catt Publications.

Chapter 5: Multicultural Relationship Competency: Case of a College Student

Our psychological understanding is most easily achieved when we observe people of our own cultural background. Their movements, verbal behavior, desires, and sensitivities are similar to our own and we are enabled to empathize with them on the basis of clues that may seem insignificant to people from a different background. Yet even when we observe people from a different culture whose experience is unlike our own, we usually trust that we will be able to understand them psychologically…. (Kohut, 1959, p. 463).

A half-century ago, Kohut (1959) eloquently referenced the significance of a common cultural heritage to the formation of empathy and, by implication, to the therapeutic relationship. In short, cultural diversity presents us with unique issues that may hinder our usual capacity to understand and connect with one another. Thus, psychologists must be aware of how cultural diversity may lead to misattunement and misunderstanding of particular significance to a therapeutic relationship.

As early as 1913, Freud explicitly acknowledged the importance of a well-developed rapport. This sentiment has remained intact despite ongoing genesis of differing theoretical perspectives and brands of therapy. More recently, the significance of the working alliance has been demonstrated by much research over the past two decades (Horvath, 2001). In particular, this research shows a positive correlation between the quality of the alliance and treatment outcome. Indeed, research has demonstrated that almost any well-planned treatment tends to be efficacious, with the therapeutic relationship accounting for more variance in efficacy than the specific therapeutic paradigm (Vasquez, 2007). Kottler (1991) emphasized that regardless of the therapeutic approach, the development of a trusting, honest, caring relationship between the client and the therapist is a universal condition for positive change.

Unique issues, however, interfere with establishing a therapeutic relationship within multicultural counseling. Multicultural dilemmas between therapists and clients may contribute to early dropout rates and/or dissatisfaction with therapy in racial and ethnic minority populations. In fact, studies have shown that in the United States (U.S.), ethnic and racial minorities are less likely to utilize mental health services and are less likely than Whites/White Americans to receive quality care when they do (Sue, 1998). A meta-analysis by Griner and Smith (2006) identified several reasons for this disparity: a) cultural differences between clinician and client, b) mistrust of services by minority clients, and c) socioeconomic limitations. First, these findings reflect that cultural differences between clients and clinicians may lead clinicians to misinterpret the experiences of their clients and thus fail to meet their needs. Second, such results suggest that culturally diverse clients may mistrust mental health services due to historic racial disparities in the United States and a shortage of therapists from their own racial, ethnic, national, or linguistic backgrounds.

In an effort to increase sensitivity and effectiveness in multicultural therapy, the multicultural competence literature (American Psychological Association [APA], 2003, 2017) has emphasized the therapist's development of cultural knowledge, skills, and awareness. Within this literature, specific skills have included therapist respect for bilingualism and culture-specific services. While a skills approach is necessary, we propose that the Multicultural Relationship Competency (MCRC), a set of interpersonal engagements that allows therapists to quickly adapt to culturally different clients and facilitate a therapy process, is necessary in advancing multiculturally competent therapy. The MCRC model defines interpersonal engagements as respectful communication processes that encourage active client participation, teamwork, complementary client-therapist interactions, and identification of and agreement on desired outcomes. Overall, interpersonal engagements help to establish and maintain a multicultural relationship.

Preceding Multicultural and Related Mainstream Models

In recent years, there have been discussions on culturally sensitive counseling that began to shape MCRC's conceptualization of what factors are essential to multicultural competent therapy. For instance, Hall (2001) argued that culturally sensitive counseling must address three constructs common in the multicultural literature: interpersonal/interdependence needs of collectivistic people, racism and discrimination experiences of People-of-Color, and spirituality/religious values that have wide-ranging influence on how people live in three quarters of the world. These three constructs are integral to the MCRM therapist's responsiveness to a client's contexts.

Additionally, D.W. Sue et al.'s (1992) call to therapists to develop appropriate multicultural techniques inspired the development of MCRC. Sue et al. stated that for multicultural competency skills, therapists must necessarily work to develop appropriate techniques for clients of different cultures. Sue et al. suggested 15 skills, including: respect for indigenous helping practices and networks; sensitivity to conflicts between counseling and cultural values; an understanding of institutional barriers; awareness of biases in assessment; understanding of family structure, hierarchies, values, and beliefs; knowledge of discriminatory practices in society and the community;

conveyance of appropriate nonverbal messages; institutional intervention; consultation with traditional healers and spiritual leaders; an interest in a client's language; appropriate use of traditional assessment with diverse clients; effort to eliminate bias, prejudice, and discrimination; and providing clients with education and information. In advancing Sue et al.'s work, MCRC focuses on the multicultural counseling relationship rather than specific skills.

The importance of the multicultural counseling relationship that is central to MCRC is also drawn from the multicultural literature. Sodowsky and her colleagues (1994, 1998) considered the multicultural counseling relationship (a 4th factorial dimension found to accompany the knowledge, skills, and awareness multicultural competency factors) to be the human element in counseling, characterized by underlying tensions of racial mistrust, fears of comparisons with a White normative group, and cultural sensitivity about confidentiality and privacy. Therapist sensitivity to a power-based relationship has been called "ethnotherapeutic empathy" by Sodowsky et al. (1998, p. 262) and entails a therapist integrating multicultural knowledge with the client's subjective experience of group specific identities. Further, a therapist's integration of multiple identities of a client with the client's individuality occurs through therapist affirmation of the unique dynamics of a diversely characterized client (Roysircar et al., 2009). Fuertes and Ponterotto (2003) said the following about the multicultural working alliance:

> ... [Therapists] are open to criticism from or to being tested by the client; and [therapists] can establish goals and formulate tasks with the client. [Therapists] are able to communicate openness to and are able to discuss issues associated with gender, race,

ethnicity, culture, socio-economic background, sexual orientation, and other human diversity factors with their clients. [Therapists] can sensitively process differences in race and culture. [Therapists] are able to name or identify for their client's experiences that may be of a racist or oppressive nature. [Therapists] are able and willing to modify their theoretical and technical styles and/or interventions to meet the client psychologically, including knowing when not to discuss race or salient cultural differences with their clients. (pp. 55-56).

A more specific therapy model that has influenced the importance of the therapeutic alliance and the establishment of the interpersonal engagements of the MCRC model is Leong and Lee's (2006) Cultural Accommodation Model (CAM). The CAM's goal is to provide a theoretical guide for counseling as well as for research on evidence-based practice with a multicultural population. The CAM puts forth the idea that clients should be seen as belonging to three different group levels. First and foremost, they are a member of humanity and thus share traits and characteristics with all people. Second, a client must be perceived in the group dimension, incorporating their ethnicity, race, gender, class, etc. Third, a client must be seen as an individual, separate and distinct from the group. Leong and Lee proposed that all clients be seen and treated in a holistic manner, with client concerns seen as universal, group-specific, and individualistic.

After determining what elements of a theory are applicable to all groups and what is specific to the White American group that results in cultural gaps, the therapist may identify concepts from the multicultural literature to fill these identified gaps (Leong & Lee, 2006). The therapist tests a new culture-specific technique to see if it is more valid than the previously unmodified technique. Leong and Lee (2006) said that failure to adapt prevalent methods may lead to disengagement and premature termination by clients. In addition, the authors of the present article argue that a therapist's culturally hindering engagement may also lead to premature termination by a multicultural client. An engagement of interpersonal connection is of the utmost importance for the therapist and multicultural client, which, in a study of counseling adolescent ESL clients resulted in positive client gains (Roysircar, 2005). Hence, the primary concern of MCRC is interpersonal engagement.

The MCRC model shares conceptual elements with relational-cultural theory (RCT), as well. RCT is a feminist psychological approach (Frey, 2013) that emphasizes the importance of connective relational experiences in promoting personal and societal growth. The importance of understanding the world through multiple perspectives is advanced by RCT, and current RCT has actively sought to incorporate cultural diversity into its research and practice. In clinical contexts, RCT requires that therapists be constantly aware of the relational patterns and patterns of disconnection of their clients, as well as those that therapists too hold. Such awareness is believed to allow therapists to anticipate and prevent replicating harmful past relationships and, in turn, provide a corrective relational experience. Furthermore, therapist empathy, responsiveness, acknowledgement of power, and acknowledgement of contribution to disconnection are proposed to enhance growth-fostering relationship in which relational scars can be healed and more authentic and healthy patterns be promoted (Jordan, 2010).

Similar to MCRC, RCT therapy is defined more by the growth-fostering relationship between the therapist and client than by techniques and interventions. More so, both

RCT and MCRC promote the ability to hold multiple perspectives or engage in Diunital/Dialectical Reasoning. Perhaps most notably, RCT and MCRC not only recognize that providing a therapeutic relationship requires active Self-Reflexivity of the therapist, but understand it to be essential in therapeutic work as well. Furthermore, elements believed to promote a growth-fostering relationship in RCT, such as responsiveness, compare to the various MCRC engagements.

The importance of the therapeutic relationship that forms the base of MCRC is seen in time-limited dynamic psychotherapy (TLDP) as well. TLDP, which arises from psychodynamic theory, suggests that clients are caught in cyclical maladaptive relational patterns. It proposes that the therapeutic relationship is an essential mechanism of change and is related to the effectiveness of treatment. Additionally, TLDP requires that therapists attend to interactional patterns that arise in session and allows for appropriate therapist self-disclosure (Levenson, 2010). MCRC's focus on the value of the therapeutic relationship, promotion of therapist attention to relationships in session, and belief that therapist self-disclosure can be used appropriately, correspond to the above-mentioned core tenants of TLDP.

Last, MCRC relates to motivational interviewing (MI). Similar to MI's "spirit" of partnership, acceptance, absolute worth, and accurate empathy (Miller & Rollnick, 2013), MCRC stresses the importance of a collaborative therapeutic process that advocates incorporating clients' own understanding within the processes of conceptualization, goal setting, and treatment formation. Also, in both of these models, integration of clients' own knowledge about themselves is regarded as an essential element in promoting therapeutic change. More so, engagement processes are a core to MI as well as MCRC. In fact, the MI's understanding of engagement is deemed to be a prerequisite to the advancing of three other processes in therapy: focusing, evoking, and planning (Miller & Rollnick, 2013).

The Five MCRC Steps

MCRC recommends that therapists relate using five steps as they meet with their culturally different clients. First, they are to find common features between them and their client: the universal common ground. Second, they approximate a cognitive match (congruence between the therapist's and client's perspectives) with their client (Sue, 1998). Third, they delve into the experiences of their client as a cultural minority individual and the client's related group-specific identities. Fourth, therapists see that the client is not only a member of a culturally different group but is indeed his or her own person with an individual identity. Fifth, therapists become collaborators with their clients, advancing the client's goals for counseling. In this way the therapist is able interact with the client in a "holistic" manner to address all parts of who the client is. While MCRC encourages using the multicultural literature to become knowledgeable, it specifically calls for the therapist to learn five interpersonal engagements to better connect with the multicultural client.

Interpersonal Engagements

MCRC draws from the ideals of the multicultural competencies, such as therapist cultural self-awareness and recognizing the worldview of the culturally different client. At the same time, MCRC offers a realistic and actual approach to clients. MCRC includes five interpersonal engagements: Affective Communication, Relationship Building, Diunital/Dialectical Reasoning, Observation of a Client's Local Contexts and Culture, and Model Management through Self-Reflexivity.

Affective Communication

The ability to speak the language of a group of people allows unique insights into the culture associated with that language. For instance, Griner and Smith's (2006) meta-analysis examined mental health interventions that were culturally adapted; in these interventions, clients who were matched on the basis of language had twice as effective outcomes than those who were not. This finding speaks to the significance of bilingual competence in therapeutic settings. However, knowing a language does not equip the speaker to practice bilingual counseling, which requires clinician's professional expertise (APA, 2017).

While being bilingual or multilingual is very helpful, therapists cannot lose sight of the affective impact of nonverbal communication. Affective Communication refers to the therapist's emotional engagement with the client, such as attending and responding to clients' affective cues. It is connecting with the client's subjective culture (e.g., values, norms, and practices that have become implicit to the client). Idiomatic and locally popular exchanges and nonverbal communications are aspects of Affective Communication. Perhaps most importantly, Affective Communication, when done well, unequivocally conveys to the client that the therapist is happy to see him or her.

Affective Communication may be expressed through humor and enjoyment of exchanges with the client or by showing concern for him or her by referring back to and remembering the client's particular contexts where stressors are located. For example, enjoying the client is exemplified by the following statement: "My second meeting was very enjoyable and I actually found myself laughing with her much of the time."

Affective Communication also includes behavioral responses of admiration, affirmation, and mirroring that take the therapy process to another level, as shown in the following example: "It was when I stated that it must have been difficult for my client not to have the support of her family and community that she would have had in India, that she began to tell me more about her tragedy. She cried and shared how the separation from her culture of birth made grieving more difficult for her."

It should be noted that, Affective Communication does not call for therapists to mimic the communication style of clients, but rather to match or align one's communication style. It asks the therapist to make a sincere attempt to conform to nonpathological behavior patterns of culturally different clients. This form of mirroring opens up the emotive and relational aspects of communication and helps the therapist to connect with the client's subjective experience of his or her culture.

While MCRC increases the therapeutic alliance, the authors keep in mind the contention that a significant part of the relationship between the therapist and client is separate from the work of therapy as well as transference-countertransference configurations. This is the personal relationship that exists from the first moment of contact between therapist and client, and if things go well, an aspect that deepens as the work progresses. This relationship has realism to it or what could be thought of as experiencing and perceiving another in an accurate manner. In the same way, Affective Communication of MCRC seeks to connect to the real person of the client.

Relationship Building

MCRC sees the therapist-client interaction process as relationship building. Through Relationship Building, a therapist supports an exchange of information and trust sufficient to allow the therapist access to the client. Relationship Building is built on therapist behaviors that lead to trust, faith, hope, and confidence in the therapist.

While Carl Rogers' core conditions of therapy, such as being warm and genuine, are necessary, they are not sufficient. In particular, Clemmont E. Vontress, an African American therapist, asserted that the core conditions are not enough in multicultural counseling. Vontress had the opportunity to meet Rogers and asked him several questions. As Vontress (2004) said:

> I asked him about the relevancy of his theory for counseling African Americans, who might feel hostile towards Whites for historical reasons. I wanted to know how empathy, therapist congruence, and positive regard....would affect the White therapist-Black client dyad. He [Rogers] replied these therapeutic ingredients would still apply if the client perceived them in the White therapist....He said nothing about how White therapists perceive Black clients. (p. iv).

Similar to Vontress, we endorse the Multicultural Counseling Competencies' recommendation that therapists become aware of their own assumptions, biases, and values concerning culturally diverse clients. Taking an active role in becoming aware of personal assumptions, biases, and values can aid in promoting respectful therapist communications based on positive interracial attitudes, thereby preventing subtle racism, stereotyped threat, and microaggressions. Trust is subsequently engendered.

Another facet of Relationship Building includes knowing what self-disclosure means in the client's culture. Therapeutic work can shift depending upon clients' cultural understandings of self-disclosure. For example, in many Asian cultures, self-disclosure of mistakes, failures, broken relationships, sexual identity, loss of employment, or ridicule is accompanied by feelings of shame and loss of face. Thus, to be consistent with the Asian values of self-control and interpersonal boundaries, MCRC therapists are sensitive to their clients' potential loss of face concerns and vulnerability through self-disclosure. Conversely, some American Indian cultures expect some degree of self-disclosure. For example, various meetings are initiated by providing all participants the opportunity to say something about themselves. In such a case, the therapist will listen respectfully as other participants speak about themselves and their experience and then say something about himself or herself; the clinician is expected to self-disclose as well. Applying the Native American clinical practice of self-disclosure, an MCRC therapist may think the following about self-disclosure: "Even though it seemed strange at first to be sharing my experiences as the granddaughter of a Polish immigrant, I realized that it was important for my client to know how I felt about ethnicity, culture, and family background: it was as if she wanted to know if she could trust me."

Therapist-client shared feedback facilitates collaboration, as indicated by the following example: "If I communicated to my client that he did not understand me, then that might affect our relationship. My response was to request him to keep asking me questions. I, then, added that if it was permissible with him, we could both check in with each other occasionally to ensure we understood each other. He agreed and this method seemed effective." In addition, Relationship Building includes identifying common experiences. This practice creates a common, universal ground for the culturally different client and therapist to meet. Examples of common experiences include those that surround children, parents, spirituality, work, recreation, and family celebrations, which are experiences of all people.

Thompson et al. (1994) showed that low levels of racial mistrust in Black clients were associated with a greater number of disclosing statements to Black therapists, whereas high levels of mistrust were associated with a lesser number of disclosing statements to White therapists. Thompson et al. thus suggested that regardless of race, therapists must contend with the mistrust of Black clients, with high levels of mistrust being related to superficial exploration and potential early termination. An example of a Caucasian American therapist broaching the issue of race is as follows: "As a Caucasian I feel quite hesitant to even bring up race. So much racism still exists in the United States that I do not wish to insult my African American client. I have witnessed so much hatred expressed because of race. But once my client and I acknowledged our different races, and when I said that racial tension is one of the biggest societal problems in the Unites States today, we both all at once felt freed, almost liberated from being silent. My client looked relieved." An MCRC therapist is comfortable initiating conversations about racial differences in a growth-enhancing way early in the multicultural relationship, notably even if the client does not seek out recognition of such differences and does not present with issues related to race or racial identity. This suggestion is in line with the writings of authors who propose a culture-specific (i.e., "emic") approach to counseling Black clients who live in a racial climate that minimizes or even questions the significance of the Black experience as a positive or growth-promoting aspect of their psychology (Thompson et al., 1994; Utsey et al., 2001).

Additionally, pacing with the client leads to Relationship Building. Therapists must be mindful of how cultural values, traditions, and understandings can subsequently affect the pace of therapeutic work. Therapists might recognize a slower pace if clients are more hesitant to discuss issues that have previously been invalidated by the majority culture, as noted by the following example, "I had so many more questions for her, but I realized that this process was going to have to proceed at her own speed. I was wondering what it must be like to be Korean and be adopted by White parents and how she could never really "hide" the fact that she was adopted. She didn't seem ready to talk about her feelings, and I did not push her." Dyche and Zayas (2001) believe that building collaborative relationships is important with populations that have often been disempowered and are distrustful of services.

Also of relevance to Relationship Building is research clarifying processes of rupture and repair in the therapeutic alliance with Japanese and South Asian clients (Roland, 2006). For example, a Japanese client's progression from withdrawal to stating concretely dissatisfaction with therapy to self-assertion of needs, and the therapist's subsequent validation of the client's therapy experiences typifies the resolution of a rupture marked by the client's initial silence. In contrast, ruptures marked by client confrontation are resolved as underlying feelings of vulnerability and the client's wishes to be nurtured; the dynamics of anger are uncovered and processed by the therapist (Roland, 2006). Similarly, alliance ruptures can also result from unintended slights or perceived as microaggressions by African American clients. Thus, part of Relationship Building includes being adept at recognizing ruptures in the therapeutic alliance and developing the necessary skills for making reparations.

Diunital/Dialectical Reasoning

The interface of opposing client and therapist worldviews requires the therapist to engage in Diunital Reasoning, the third engagement. Described by Myers (1988), Diunital (day vs. night) Reasoning is a cognitive flexibility or capacity for cognitive complexity in recognizing the reality inherent in two competing or even exclusionary worldviews. Diunital Reasoning leads to the acceptance of others' worldviews as legitimate, even when different from the therapist's. This Reasoning then progresses to the acceptance of these other worldviews as legitimate representations of the experiences of cultural groups. Ultimately, the therapist comes to recognize that a particular worldview both accounts for and explains the experience of an individual client. Indeed, such ability to hold multiple perspectives is becoming increasingly important. In a meta-analysis of studies examining mental health interventions that were culturally adapted, 84% explicitly included interventions with cultural values and concepts (Griner & Smith, 2006) that were not common to the worldview of European Americans.

This third MCRC engagement requires that the therapist hold the tension between two opposing beliefs, even when the therapist's perspective is threatened. The therapist understands and accepts a client's worldview as ultimately meaningful for that client as his or her reality. For example, in Diunital Reasoning, a therapist would recognize the legitimacy of spiritual- or religious-based healing in spite of the fact that an indigenous approach and the European American medical model of healing include competing concepts regarding not only "how" to heal, but 'what' healing itself is.

Diunital Reasoning involves the notion of cognitive match (Sue, 1998). The process of Diunital Reasoning allows therapists to remain open to various viewpoints that their clients subscribe to. For example, Martínez-Taboas (2005) asked a Puerto Rican client how she explained her psychogenic seizures, showing respect for her worldview of spiritist beliefs. The client's treatment goal was to confront the spirit of her grandmother, who had committed suicide, and free herself from guilt and fear. This goal was accomplished through many sessions of the empty chair technique. Martínez-Taboas integrated these experiential techniques with cognitive behavior therapy. This case study illustrates the benefits of a cultural conceptualization that takes into account the client's religious attributions with regard to her illness and describes how the effectiveness of traditional therapeutic modalities (cognitive-behavioral in this case) can be enhanced by reframing symptoms from the client's worldview.

Diunital Reasoning represents a key cognitive skill in MCRC that allows a therapist to accept the culturally specific views of clients without having to abandon his or her own worldview. In the practice of Diunital Reasoning, therapists do not change their worldview while interpersonally engaged; rather, "The capacity to face others with openness to their reality while simultaneously maintaining coherence in your own beliefs and sense of self is the dialectic process behind human attachment and social contract" (Dyche & Zayas, 2001, p. 257). Therapists maintaining their own view while respecting their client's view is given an illustration here: "First, I am prompted to think of ways in which I could either address or alter the confrontational, straightforwardness of my African-American female client. But that would be changing my client to be like me. Gradually, I reasoned that my less direct approach represents who I am, and as long as I am sincere, my client and I can still communicate. I might even learn from her how to be less ambiguous, to speak less in "maybes," and I would then prevent mixed messages. My client can learn from me how speaking "nicely" can also go a long way interpersonally."

Observing a Client within Local Contexts and Culture

Understanding the customs and practices of another culture is a major challenge. Therapists can use a number of resources to develop an understanding of the customs and practices of a culture. However, any of these knowledge resources may provide information that does not accurately describe the practices of a particular subgroup and may apply even less to an individual within the larger group or a subset of the group.

As a way to avoid stereotyping, therapists may observe clients within their local cultures by asking them to share their understanding of a particular behavior from the perspective of their local community. The client could be asked to describe the community's expected reaction(s) to the behavior. The therapist, thus, observes a client's understanding of his or her culture. By treating a minority client as an individual functioning within various contexts, the therapist views culture as being local, subjective, in flux, highly heterogeneous, and as having permeable boundaries.

Lakes, et al., (2006) suggest that clinicians discern what is at stake in the client's local social world to determine what is culturally important to the client and thus what to focus on in therapy. Incorporating the client's perspective allows an understanding of the client's individual experience of a context. The client is empowered, and a collaborative spirit is promoted. Clinicians are better able to cross cultural divides by recognizing the importance of their clients' local worldview, family supports, community, and religious group. In addition, individual identity is interwoven with familial and social structures because family and social hierarchies and loyalties typically remain powerful throughout a client's lifetime in a collectivistic culture.

Observation consists of three assessment steps. Identifying patterns of culture-based behaviors includes, first, the therapist's recognition that a certain behavior is "different." Second, the therapist identifies the client's worldview that underlies the behavior. The identification of worldview consists of asking the client about the meaning, purpose, or value of the behavior. Third, the therapist asks clients to describe their understanding of the behavior in their community and the community's reaction to the client's behavior. Such Observation is especially important because if therapists do not know how a reference group views the behavior, they will interpret the behavior based on their own worldview, thus providing biased assessment. Observation of a client's culture is provided in the following example: "My client comes from a culture where an extended family like a grandmother or an aunt works together with the mother to care for children. But here, as an immigrant in the United States, my client does not have an extended family. The management of her workplace does not approve of her bringing a child to work even if she thinks it to be in the child's best interest. I, on the other hand, understood why my client cannot just leave her children alone at home—even with a babysitter. I am validating in the here-and-now my client's value-based parenting decisions."

Model Management through Self-Reflexivity

Self-Reflexivity is a heightened level of self-awareness in which curiosity and examination engender a meta-analytic understanding of one's behaviors. Although all of the interpersonal engagements inform the multiculturally competent therapist, Self-Reflexivity is the core of multicultural competency development. Self-Reflexivity manages all the interpersonal engagements as a coherent whole because it is a thread that runs through every engagement. Through Self-Reflexivity, therapists at their core learn to become comfortable in their own skin. Therapists intimately know their own story. Pederson's (1994) notion of therapists listening to internal dialogues is one aspect of Self-Reflexivity. In Pederson's Triad Training model, therapists monitor their own internal dialogue as well as attend to the anti-therapist and the pro-therapist, which are the client's negative and positive help-seeking attitudes.

During the interpersonal engagements, therapists spend time being introspective about personal reactions based on their own worldview and cultural socialization. Therapists hypothesize about their own assumptions, values, and biases when challenged by the views and behaviors of culturally different clients. New self-views and views of others develop creating an enrichment of ideas, alternatives, and explanations.

One of the differences between the awareness called for in MCRC and the awareness of attitudes and beliefs called for in the multicultural competencies (Sue et al., 1992) is the active nature of the awareness in Self-Reflexivity. Whereas the multicultural competencies ask therapists to cultivate awareness of their own assumptions, values, and biases, MCRC calls for therapists to become process-oriented, to be aware of their engagements with clients, and to continually assess these engagements through the lens of Self-Reflexivity.

Self-Reflexivity gives therapists a basis for continuous self-assessment (Author, 2004). The following is an example of self-reflection: "My discussion with my British international student client provided me many opportunities to become very aware of the American ideals that I have inherited. My family has always had guns and most of us enjoy target shooting, so guns have been commonplace in my life. My discussion with my client prompted me to analyze gun ownership from a cultural perspective (e.g., the American cowboy image, hunting in rural areas, and the U.S. second amendment giving the right to bear arms); as well as from my familial outdoor sports orientation. For the first time, I was reflecting on gun ownership in comparison to the experiences of someone raised in another country, where even the police do not carry guns."

MCRC as a Whole

One might think of MCRC as a circle (see Figure 3), with each of the interpersonal engagements fused with the others and forming a whole. Failure to employ one of the engagements compromises the other engagements, and, consequently, the multicultural relationship; this significantly reduces one's ability to conduct culturally sensitive practice. The interpersonal engagements of MCRC are interlocking and interdependent. As an example, a therapist's skillful use of Affective Communication facilitates Relationship Building. Furthermore, the ability to use Diunital Reasoning and thereby accept the plurality of values and beliefs that both clients and therapists bring to therapy frees therapists from feelings of hypocrisy (or political correctness) and thus, generates a genuine interaction. Therapists are responsive to a client's culture by particularizing client behaviors within the client's interpersonal contexts at the micro level of a large social geography and societal system. At a metacognitive level, therapists step outside of themselves to monitor and examine their engagements in a self-reflective and self-corrective feedback loop. Figure 3 illustrates the MCRC model.

Case Illustration—Aziza

The following case was developed by Dr. Jill Lee-Barber, Director of the University Counseling and Testing Center, Georgia State University, Atlanta. Client anonymity is protected with slants in contextual details, while still maintaining the realness of the client.

Aziza is a nineteen-year-old heterosexual, Muslim, sophomore woman student in a university. Aziza immigrated to the United States from Bangladesh with her parents when she was five years of age. She is the fifth of six children of her father and the older of the two from his current wife, Aziza's mother. Aziza's father owns a small profitable business. The family regularly travels to Bangladesh to visit relatives and engage in business ventures. Aziza was reluctantly allowed to leave the family home and reside in university housing with roommates whom the family had known for many years within the Bangladeshi community. Regular weekend visits were expected of Aziza with large family meals.

Figure 3. *Multicultural Relationship Competency Model*

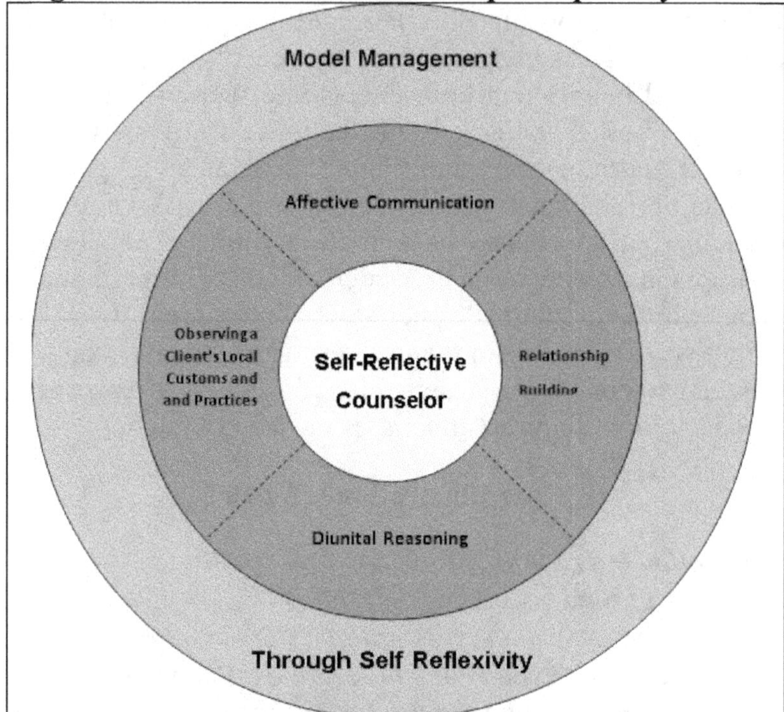

Note: The interpersonal engagements of MCRC are interlocking and interdependent.

The therapist identifies as a middle-aged, White, United Methodist, married, lesbian mother. She has practiced in university counseling centers for nearly twenty years. The therapist was raised near a metropolitan city in Southern United States. She was raised living near her extended family, including grandparents, aunts, uncles, and cousins. In this context, weekly large family meals were expected. The therapist's family of origin can be described as conservative Christian. Her mother was a retired ES elementary school teacher and has adopted siblings of African nationalities, who participate in the large extended family as well.

During her freshman year, Aziza began to experiment with her new freedom and attended fraternity parties with friends; she also began drinking alcohol for the first time, which is forbidden by her Islamic faith. Aziza presented to the university counseling center on a crisis walk-in basis and reported that she woke up after a party with an American male friend having sex with her. She reported that she told him "no" and that she cried and begged him to stop. Aziz tearfully reported that she is expected to be a virgin until marriage. She described that she had not been sleeping well, could not concentrate, had very little appetite, and had nightmares about the incident. Aziza did not want to report this to the university officials, and she believed that she could not tell anyone about this event. She blamed herself for going to the party, for drinking, for not choosing "worthy" friends, and for living on campus when her parents would have preferred she live at home. Aziza believed she would never be happy again and that she must carry this shame and secret alone.

The initial facts Aziza shared were: she would never report the incident to the police or university officials and that her parents and sister could never know what happened to her. She described a duty not to "cause her parents any hurt" and as a daughter not to "soil her family's name." Furthermore, Aziza was protecting herself from her parents' anger as she was expecting to be punished and made to leave college. She did not want her sister to be burdened with knowing that something this horrible can happen. Additionally, Aziza believed that she was supposed to forgive the male student who attacked her. She stated that this was a part of her spiritual practice and that her father had forgiven people for "worse" like murders of family members owing to religious differences.

Personal Reflection Questions

- To what behaviors (individual, interpersonal, and group dynamics) do I feel most empathically attuned?
- How might my natural attunement and empathy be reflective of my personal culture(s)?
- What common cultural practices are difficult for me to find empathy and/or understanding? How has this manifested in my work?

Discussion Questions Related to Aziza

- How might Aziza's intersectional identities be conceptualized as protective factors? How might her intersectional identities be conceptualized as vulnerabilities?
- How many relationships do you consider when thinking about Aziza's story? What are these relationships, and why are they important in your conceptualizing?

MCRC Model Application

Below is the application of the MCRC with the example of Aziza. It is divided by the MCRC five interpersonal engagements.

Applying Affective Communication to Counseling Case

Affective Communication facilitates the personal relationship that exists from the first moment of contact between the therapist and the client, and if things go well, an aspect that deepens as the work progresses. This is the intangible seed of connection that can grow into a healing relationship or not. In Aziza's case, during the initial phase of therapy, the therapist focused on creating a safe space in which Aziza could speak her truth at her own pace about the incident to a person who she knew would not tell university officials or her family. The therapist was warm with Aziza and encouraged her to share only the parts of her story with which she felt comfortable. In addition, the therapist has a tea pot in her office and offered Aziza tea each visit. Notably, Aziza asked if the therapist would have tea with her. The therapist joined Aziza for a cup of tea each visit. It seemed important not to decline this simple act of communion which began Affective Communication with this client. The therapist supported Aziza in her need to keep the incident private and discuss it only in therapy, stating that the therapist believed that Aziza needed to be in control of who knew about this event, how much, and when.

Affective Communication continued as the therapist affirmed the dilemma of having spiritual and familial expectations of forgiveness and being a good person and then having something so painful happen that one wonders how this evil could be possible. Aziza then shared with the therapist that according to the Quran she cannot expect the forgiveness of Allah if she does not forgive those who have wronged her. She further shared that in Islam, one is even expected to forgive one's enemies. This act of forgiveness is quite similar to the teachings of Jesus that have been central to the therapist since childhood. The therapist validated the dilemma of having a spiritual belief about forgiveness that is challenged by deep personal suffering caused by another person. Of note, Affective Communication with individuals from the majority of the world's cultures can include a support of the importance of people's religion or spirituality.

Applying Relationship Building to Counseling Case

Relationship Building resulted from Affective Communication. The client's ambivalence about therapy was expressed through multiple appointment cancellations or last-minute requests to reschedule. The therapist responded to these with personal phone calls to follow up with the client and inquire about her well-being. Later, the client told the therapist that these calls caused the client to believe that the therapist really cared about her and not just about a student appointment. She said that she felt that the therapist truly wanted to know that she was "okay."

Additionally, during the Relationship Building engagement, the therapist shared with the client that while she understood that Aziza did not want to tell her mother or her sister about her pain because she wanted to protect them as well as to avoid punishment and loss of face, the therapist, on the other hand, felt that if Aziza were her own daughter or sister, she would want to know and would want to help. The therapist acknowledged that listening to Aziza she realized that she and Aziza came from different cultures with sometimes complicated and nuanced meanings and consequences of disclosing about sexual assault. However, if the therapist's own daughter were harmed, as a mother she would hope to be able to help her. The therapist added that she imagined that Aziza was precious to her family, and whether they ever knew about her rape or not, that they would not want her to be suffering. At this point, Aziza began to cry. She told the therapist that her name means precious. Of note, she did not cancel further therapy appointments.

It is important to note that the therapist's self-disclosure about being a mother of a daughter was not without a great deal of thought. While acknowledging that a woman's rape has different meanings for a Muslim family and a European American family, the therapist reiterated that those who love Aziza like her mother and sister would want her to be protected, helped, nurtured, and healthy. The therapist focused on empowering Aziza with choices about what, whom, and when to ask for help. Many sessions later in the process, Aziza was able to imagine "those who have loved her the most" surrounding her in the therapy room. Aziza then imagined what they would say to her if they knew that someone had hurt her and violated her trust. She imagined what those trusted elders and her sister would want the university to do on her behalf.

After this visualization exercise, Aziza knew for sure what she wanted to do. She did not tell her family about the assault other than in her own visualization of them listening and supporting her. She decided to report the assault to the university with hopes that the man who raped her could be held accountable. She stated that her entire family would want a form of retribution, referring to myths of retribution from the Bangladeshi Muslim culture. She also stated that part of the reason her family immigrated with their children was for educational opportunities in the United States; even though she had veered away from traditional Bangladeshi Muslim values, she was beginning to feel she deserved protection to continue her education.

Applying Diunital/Dialectical Reasoning to Counseling Case

Diunital/Dialectical Reasoning frees the therapist to accept the culturally specific views of her client without having to abandon her own worldview. In this case, the therapist identifies as a White American feminist, mother of a daughter, and a university psychologist/administrator. In general, she has a bias towards reporting sexual assault so that perpetrators are identified accurately and held accountable. Additionally, in general, she has a bias towards encouraging and empowering assault survivors to share their stories with supportive others because empirical data and clinical experience demonstrate that such sharing is beneficial to the survivor. The therapist knows many university judicial boards fail to hold perpetrators accountable and that the process of reporting and formal legal procedures for survivors of sexual assault can be grueling. She is further aware of the need for a survivor to be empowered to make her own choices about when, whom, and how much to tell. Knowledge of her own biases and views and the desire to learn Aziza's worldview about her private self and public self as well as her own individualistic views about sexual assault were essential in this therapeutic work.

The decision to report her assault was not a simple one for Aziza, even after she became clear that she wanted to do it. Aziza did not believe that the university judicial system or any U.S. system would help an immigrant woman of color who was accusing an American white male. She pondered whether it would be possible to both report the assault, to vindicate her honor and prevent the man from assaulting another person, as well as to continue to work with her spiritual practice of eventual forgiveness. She worried about never being able to feel like a "normal college student" again. She longed to feel carefree and trusting again but doubted that she ever would. She did not believe that reporting the sexual assault would bring normal happiness back to her. In this phase of therapy, the therapist engaged in Diunital/Dialectical Reasoning; while the therapist is aware of the consequences that can occur for women who report sexual assault, she did not share Aziza's view that reporting the assault to university officials would not be helpful to her. The therapeutic process focused on empowering Aziza to make her own decision about reporting her assault and on recognizing that the views and beliefs of both an immigrant Muslim college student client and a European American middle aged feminist therapist could each co-exist and be valid.

Applying Observing a Client within Local Contexts and Culture to Counseling Case

Aziza described that in her Bangladeshi Muslim community she was expected to be a virgin until marriage and that revealing her sexual assault to her parents would cause them concern about her worth in the "marriage market." She was certain that the assault would be blamed on her within the community because she had left the family home to live independently, essentially against her parents' wishes. The belief that her community and family might say "we told you so" about the risks of independence and living on a typical American university campus was what kept Aziza feeling isolated in her pain.

With her imagination of her grandmother's presence and that of her sisters, cousins, and her mother, Aziza was able to feel strengthened and sure that this network of women would not have wanted her to be raped by a drunk American "friend" while she was new to living in a dormitory. She said that she knew that if her circle of beloved women knew, they would insist that "justice be done." The therapist understood that what the women in Aziza's family would want made Aziza stronger even though she also understood that Aziza believed that the consequences of directly talking with them about it would be too great. Aziza said that eventually she wanted her younger sister to know about what had happened so that her sister could protect herself and that if Aziza were to tell her the story, she would want her sister to know that she had reported it so that the perpetrator could possibly be punished. In these ways, Aziza's local community was brought into therapy.

Applying Model Management through Self-Reflexivity to Counseling Case

The skill of model management through Self-Reflexivity requires not only multicultural self-awareness, but an active commitment to remain engaged in the process of introspection about one's own worldview and its impact on interactions with others. The skill of Self-Reflexivity is characterized by the cognitive process of curiosity and the ability to step outside of oneself with critical mindedness, as well as the affective process of humility and vulnerability. The therapist engaged in this reflective practice. She reflected on her European American and feminist values, biases, and assumptions. She did judicious self-disclosure in order to find a common ground with Aziza and facilitate relationship-building and Affective Communication. This required a dynamic awareness of self and the client with regard to how much disclosure would be helpful to Aziza. The circle of MCRC interactive engagements was managed by a self-evaluation process, so that the therapy evidenced therapist self-corrections and cultural conceptualization and not her agenda of explicit or implicit biases.

Conclusion

It is imperative that therapists recognize the necessity of actively pursuing multicultural relational competence. While recent decades have brought theoretical and research advances both confirming and emphasizing the importance of the therapeutic relationship, cultural diversity presents us with unique issues that may hamper our usual capacity to understand and connect therapeutically. Hence, attending to the misattunements and misunderstandings that may often result from cultural diversity is of particular importance to avert the ruptures that are deleterious to the therapy process. In this chapter, we have argued for an emphasis on the

Multicultural Relationship Competency (MCRC) model and proposed five interpersonal engagements: Affective Communication, Relationship Building, Diunital/Dialectical Reasoning, Observation of Clients within their Local Contexts and Cultures, and Model Management through Self-Reflexivity. These engagements are common to all people and not necessarily skills-specific to one theoretical approach to therapy. The MCRC model draws upon the ideals of the multicultural competencies, such as therapist cultural self-awareness and recognition of client worldview. Furthermore, this model offers a practical approach to developing a strong multicultural relationship with diverse clients.

It is essential that we are able to provide competent services to our clients. Fostering a multiculturally therapeutic relationship is vital to the therapeutic outcomes of culturally diverse clients. It is our hope that the MCRC model will enhance and promote the therapeutic relational experience for a range of clients.

References

American Psychological Association. (2003). Guidelines on multicultural education, training, research, practice, and organizational change for psychologists. *American Psychologist, 58*(5), 377-402. https://doi.org/10.1037/0003-066x.58.5.377

American Psychological Association. (2017). Multicultural guidelines: An ecological approach to context, identity, and intersectionality, 2017. *PsycEXTRA Dataset.* https://doi.org/10.1037/e501962018-001

Dyche, L., & Zayas, L. H. (2001). Cross-cultural empathy and training the contemporary psychotherapist. *Clinical Social Work Journal, 29*(3), 245-258. https://doi.org/10.1023/a:1010407728614

Frey, L. L. (2013). Relational-cultural therapy: Theory, research, and application to counseling competencies. *Professional Psychology: Research and Practice, 44*(3), 177-185. https://doi.org/10.1037/a0033121

Fuertes, J. N., & Ponterotto, J. G. (2003). Culturally appropriate intervention strategies. In G. Roysircar, P. Arrendondo, J. N. Fuertes, J. G. Ponterotto, & R. L. Toporek (Eds.), *Multicultural counseling competencies 2003: Association for multicultural counseling and development* (pp. 51-58). American Counseling Association.

Griner, D., & Smith, T. B. (2006). Culturally adapted mental health intervention: A meta-analytic review. *Psychotherapy: Theory, Research, Practice, Training, 43*(4), 531-548. https://doi.org/10.1037/0033-3204.43.4.531

Hall, G. C. (2001). Psychotherapy research with ethnic minorities: Empirical, ethical, and conceptual issues. *Journal of Consulting and Clinical Psychology, 69*(3), 502-510. https://doi.org/10.1037/0022-006x.69.3.502

Horvath, A. O. (2001). The alliance. *Psychotherapy: Theory, Research, Practice, Training, 38*(4), 365-372. https://doi.org/10.1037/0033-3204.38.4.365

Jordan, J. V. (2010). *Relational-cultural therapy.* American Psychological Association.

Kohut, H. (1959). Introspection, empathy, and psychoanalysis an examination of the relationship between mode of observation and theory. *Journal of the American Psychoanalytic Association, 7*(3), 459-483. https://doi.org/10.1177/000306515900700304

Kottler, J. A. (1991). *The compleat therapist.* Jossey-Bass.

Lakes, K., López, S. R., & Garro, L. C. (2006). Cultural competence and psychotherapy: Applying anthropologically informed conceptions of culture. *Psychotherapy: Theory, Research, Practice, Training, 43*(4), 380-396. https://doi.org/10.1037/0033-3204.43.4.380

Leong, F. T., & Lee, S. (2006). A cultural accommodation model for cross-cultural psychotherapy: Illustrated with the case of Asian Americans. *Psychotherapy: Theory, Research, Practice, Training, 43*(4), 410-423. https://doi.org/10.1037/0033-3204.43.4.410

Levenson, H. (2010). *Brief dynamic therapy.* American Psychological Association.

Martínez-Taboas, A. (2005). Psychogenic seizures in an Espiritismo context: The role of culturally sensitive psychotherapy. *Psychotherapy: Theory, Research, Practice, Training, 42*(1), 6-13. https://doi.org/10.1037/0033-3204.42.1.6

Miller, W. R., & Rollnick, S. (2013). *Motivational interviewing: Helping people change* (3rd ed.). Guilford Press.

Myers, L. J. (1988). *Understanding an Afrocentric world view: Introduction to an optimal psychology.* Kendall Hunt Publishing Company.

Pedersen, P. (1994). Simulating the client's internal dialogue as a counselor training technique. *Simulation & Gaming, 25*(1), 40-50. https://doi.org/10.1177/1046878194251005

Roysircar, G., Dobbins, J. E., & Malloy, K. (2009). Diversity competence in training and clinical practice. In M. Kenkel & R. Peterson (Eds.), *Competency-based education for professional psychology* (pp. 179-197). American Psychological Association.

Roysircar, G., Gard, G., Hubbell, R., & Ortega, M. (2005). Development of counseling trainees' multicultural awareness through mentoring English as a second language students. *Journal of Multicultural Counseling and Development, 33*(1), 17-36. https://doi.org/10.1002/j.2161-1912.2005.tb00002.x

Sodowsky, G. R., Kuo-Jackson, P. Y., Richardson, M. F., & Corey, A. T. (1998). Correlates of self-reported multicultural competencies: Counselor multicultural social desirability, race, social inadequacy, locus of control racial ideology, and multicultural training. *Journal of Counseling Psychology, 45*(3), 256-264. https://doi.org/10.1037/0022-0167.45.3.256

Sodowsky, G. R., Taffe, R. C., Gutkin, T. B., & Wise, S. L. (1994). Development of the multicultural counseling inventory: A self-report measure of multicultural competencies. *Journal of Counseling Psychology, 41*(2), 137-148. https://doi.org/10.1037/0022-0167.41.2.137

Sue, D. W., Arredondo, P., & McDavis, R. J. (1992). Multicultural counseling competencies and standards: A call to the profession. *Journal of Multicultural Counseling and Development, 20*(2), 64-88. https://doi.org/10.1002/j.2161-1912.1992.tb00563.x

Sue, S. (1998). In search of cultural competence in psychotherapy and counseling. *American Psychologist, 53*(4), 440-448. https://doi.org/10.1037/0003-066x.53.4.440

Thompson, C. E., Worthington, R., & Atkinson, D. R. (1994). Counselor content orientation, counselor race, and Black women's cultural mistrust and self-disclosures. *Journal of Counseling Psychology, 41*(2), 155-161. https://doi.org/10.1037/0022-0167.41.2.155

Utsey, S. O., Bolden, M. A., & Brown, A. L. (2001). Visions of revolution from the spirit Frantz Fanon: A psychology of liberation for counseling African Americans confronting societal racism and oppression. In J. G. Ponterotto, J. M. Casas, L. A. Suzuki, & C. M. Alexander (Eds.), *Handbook of multicultural counseling*. SAGE Publications.

Vasquez, M. J. (2007). Cultural difference and the therapeutic alliance: An evidence-based analysis. *American Psychologist, 62*(8), 878-885. https://doi.org/10.1037/0003-066x.62.8.878

Vontress, C. R. (2004). Forward. In R. Moodley, C. Lago, & A. Talahite (Eds.), *Carl Rogers counsels a Black client: Race and culture in person-centred counselling*. P C C S Books.

Conclusion

Colonization is normalizing the values and behaviors of an established receiving culture with immigrants from culturally stigmatized cultures of color, as illustrated in the cases of Maya and Fatima, who are religiously different South Asian immigrants in the United States. Colonization is also the imposing of imperialism on economically struggling nations defeated with military power and trade wars. Colonial change occurs in belief systems, language, art, religion, wealth distribution, social relations, education, and knowledge generation. Social attitudes of cisgenderism and heteronormativity of a dominating belief system are linked to specific stigmatization processes at community and individual levels for sexual minority individuals, such as in the case of Linda, who concealed her sexual identity in her military occupational setting and Mexican American family, both with high levels of structural stigma about gender roles.

Colonization of global mental health, under the guise of international psychology (i.e., working with foreigners), has infiltrated the academic process of cross-cultural research, training, and practice rather than locating itself within the particulars of a nationality setting, such as a different language, and its culture-specific and local goals. The *POC Casebook* has recognized the colonization of White/White American psychology, and questioned how it has infiltered our thinking, science, writing, and clinical work with a stance of superiority, stereotype threat, and implicit bias.

To deny that race or skin color is a social construct is to deny the reality of racism, as experienced by a college-going Black man, Kevin, described in this casebook. Indigenous American people had to assimilate, lest they be eradicated, which is addressed in the case analysis of Arnold. The messages of the dominating society have often been disguised as a benefit to the colonized society, selling the adaptation to colonizers as a way to access resources, social rights, acceptance, and security, which are, in fact, mistruths, with no regard for risks to mental health from the trauma of colonization and racism.

While experimental research methods and measurement seem like a strong foundation for "good research with internal validity," it is the theoretical underpinnings of a research design less concerned with external validity and generalizability to the larger population. The way data are presented statistically and in APA writing style perpetuate colonialism. It is on the back of perceived "evidence" that quantitative American methodology maintains its power and alleged superiority. Franz Fanon's *Black Skin, White Masks* (1963) was denied as a doctoral dissertation for being heretical and scandalous and is now a critical text for anti-colonial work. Fanon emphasized that decolonizing the mind was a core component to liberation from internalized Whiteness. Harold A. Franklin, the first African American student to enroll at Auburn University, successfully defended his master's thesis in history--which he wrote in 1969, 51 years ago--in March 2020. After spending over four years researching and writing a thesis, Franklin began submitting his work to his advisors. Each time he would bring it back for review, his committee would find something wrong with it. This happened multiple times. His advisors continually rejected his work on increasingly flimsy grounds. "They justified [it by saying] mine had to be perfect," Franklin said. "The other theses, they weren't perfect, so why does mine have to be perfect?" Eventually, Franklin realized that no amount of revision, correction, or resubmission would overcome the blatant prejudice he was being forced to confront. "It kept going on so long, I said, 'Hell, what you're telling me is that I won't get a degree from Auburn,'" Franklin said. "Anyway, I won a scholarship to the University of Denver and got my master's," and Franklin went on to become a college professor (https://www.theplainsman.com/article/2020/03/harold-franklin).

In the Preface, you were asked as a reader to consider using the following prompts to explore personal values, assumptions, biases, and opinions. At post-reading, we request you to self-reflect on the same questions and note whether there have been changes in your perspectives.

Personal Reflection Prompts

- In reading a vignette first, what details stand out to me as "important"? Why do these points seem important to me?
- After reading the literature review, am I drawn to a specific conceptual model? Am I resistant to a suggested conceptualization? Why might that be?
- Does any vignette remind me of something personal? How has that shaped how I engage with the material?
- What additional research would help me better understand a case presentation?
- How do I apply the suggested literature into my work with clients who experience the tensions and fluidity of intersectional identities? Are the problems arising from intersectional identities summative? How do I generalize the research on "similar" populations to clients I serve?
- What types of intersectionality am I most drawn to? How does that strengthen my work? How does it inhibit my work? Is there something about myself and my community that might draw me to a particular intersectionality?
- What are my intersectional identities? How do these shape my work?

Appendix A: Experiential Activities

The Token Game

Type of Activity: 90-minute workshop

Educational Objectives
- Increasing awareness of power and the choices that privileged people have
- Experiences related to obtaining or losing power
- Relating the Token Game to key concepts and real-life examples

Students must learn to understand privilege and the special rights, benefits, or advantages some people receive simply by having membership in a certain racial, social, or gender group and its relationship to power and oppression. *The Token Game* incorporates several concepts related to the systemic bases of individual and group interactions in an effort to provide students a chance to experience and observe pervasive forces in a safe, structured learning environment. *The Token Game* creates a social microcosm focused on power and the experience of low access for those who do not have power. *The Token Game* allows a simulation that brings out dynamics of oppression, allows for a contained personal and group involvement, and includes the appropriate level of safety for students to make sense of experiences of power.

Procedures

The experiential starts when an arbitrary pop quiz is enforced in an authoritarian manner. The quiz is composed of questions from the *Dove Counterbalance General Intelligence Test* (Dove, 1968). Group members are designated to Group 1 and Group 2, and each group remains on their side of the room.

Participating in the game

A heads-or-tails coin toss decides the "winning" group, which is Group 1. Three tokens given to each member of Group 1, and members of Group 2 receive no tokens. The instructor says that those students who hold two or more tokens will automatically receive a score of 100% on the quiz. Those students holding less than two tokens will receive the score that is earned. The group members get to decide who will get 100%. Once students have realized there are insufficient tokens for everyone to get a score of 100%, they use multiple tactics and interactions to receive, give up, or retain tokens. The instructor can respond to certain situations with simple statements such as, "That would be considered cheating, and those who cheat will automatically get zero in the quiz." The instructor and her monitors observe the interactions and discreetly keep process notes, which will be discussed in debriefing.

Debriefing and processing the game

This final step of debriefing is important as some students are surprised by their and others' actions. Processing this activity involves: (a) informing students that no score or penalty is attached to the quiz or to their performance during the game; (b) asking students what concepts they think the game was intended to highlight; (c) informing them the game centers around power and its influence on our behaviors, beliefs, and self-concept; and (d) conveying to students that their actions in the game were not intended to judge the character of any one person but rather simulate a situation to recreate what actions can emerge from an oppressive system. These points create rich opportunities to address emotions and generate meaning around social interactions that are shaped by systemically-enforced power and should not be ignored.

More specific discussion includes what it was like when students learned about the conditions for their quiz scores; how they felt when put in the one-up or one-down situation; and what were some first thoughts when realizing that chosen students would get 100%. Specific questions will be addressed to each group, usually starting with the group that had tokens at the start and then moving to the non-token group. Questions surrounding the decisions and methods of giving or receiving tokens and the feelings of power or disempowerment surrounding each will be addressed. Questions will include: Which group had to act first? Who did most of the talking? Who declined to speak? What methods were used to gain tokens or to persuade others to give up tokens? What thoughts and feelings motivated the responses? These questions also allow an opportunity to address uncomfortable feelings experienced by students and to normalize those experiences. At the same time, processing gives students a chance to examine their own responses and value judgments that they experienced.

Questions are then guided back to the large group to tie the activity to real-world examples. What actions and attitudes did students engage in that are similar to those of people who are continually oppressed and those people who tend to hold more power? Students make connections about how the activity made them feel and how it might feel in the real world

Processing the quiz is an important piece in examining another level of power and bias, and also shifts the attention to an easier, less stressful subject. The quiz is scored, which often provides impromptu opportunities for student dialogue about the different questions, many of which relate to cultural experiences outside of their own knowledge. This process provides an opportunity to highlight how their test performance theoretically could have been used to make decisions about their educational and occupational placement and also to make judgments about their ability to succeed.

Developing Cultural Awareness: Using Stories to Transcend Cultural Boundaries

Type of Activity: 1-2 Hour Workshop

Educational Objectives
- Using cross-cultural storytelling to increase multicultural awareness
- Developing cultural empathy
- Aiding participants in gaining understanding and discovering personal meaning

Discussion of cross-cultural myths can increase cultural awareness. Around the world, we are taught lessons and morals through myths. Individuals develop personal myths as a way to clarify where they have been, make meaning of what they are doing, and influence where they are going. Stories can be used in experiential training to bring textbook knowledge to life. In this workshop, participants form small groups, and each group discusses and reflects upon one story and, subsequently, creates its own group myth. Upon returning to the large group, participants share their group's experiences, reflections, and group myth. Small group activity is facilitated by guidelines, questions, and a group facilitator.

Procedures

Divide participants into small groups. Instruct participants to develop a myth that encapsulates a value, tradition, or traditional narrative of a culture. This might be a culture that they create from their imagination, or a culture or subculture that they wish to highlight. Facilitators might pose the suggested prompts to help participants develop their myth. Once the myths are developed, have the participants share their stories with the group. Below is an example of a myth.

Prompts to Aid in Developing a Myth

- Your myth should reflect the values of your chosen/created culture.
- Give a name to your culture.
- The myth should have a main character.
- There must be a supernatural element that interacts with the main character.
- The main character faces a very difficult challenge, dilemma, or conflict.
- Resolving the challenge is not easy, but a way is found to resolve the issue at hand.
- Morality is represented by the dispensation of a reward or punishment.
- You might include themes of power vs. powerlessness, rich versus poor, good versus evil, cruelty versus kindness, etc.
- Gender roles of your culture need to be included.
- Romance and various relationships may be included.
- The theme of survival, resilience, a happy ending, or a sad ending ought to be considered as an element of your myth.

Discussion

Once the participants have created their myths, they can rejoin the larger space and share their myths. Discussion might occur immediately after each participant shares a myth, however there should also be a discussion after all myths are shared that discusses the larger themes (e.g., individuality, personal coping, universal humanity) of values and meaning-making through storytelling. Below are some potential discussion questions.

<table>
<tr><td align="center">Discussion Questions for Myths</td></tr>
</table>

- How is the main character influenced by their cultural heritage? (cultural contexts)
- What is your awareness of the culture-specific values that are held by the characters in the myth or are represented by the myth? (cultural contexts)
- How do you find the myth universal? Explain how certain problems, relationships, behaviors, or environmental issues transcend cultural boundaries. (universal humanity)
- How did you personally identify with the main character's struggles? (individuality/personal empathy)
- If you had the main character's problem, how would you resolve it? (individuality/personal coping)

Example: Savitri and Satyavan, an Example of a Folk Tale from India

Once upon a time, there was a king and a queen who gave birth to a beautiful daughter named Savitri. When Savitri was old enough to marry, her father said to her, "My wonderful daughter, it is time for you to start your own family. Is there a man you would like to marry?"

Savitri knew of no man she wanted to marry, so she searched all the cities in the land. Still, she found no man she wanted to marry. Next, she searched all of the forests in the land. When Savitri came to the last forest, she happened across a young man who was chopping wood. "What is your name and what do you do?" Savitri asked the young man.

"My name is Satyavan and every morning I cut wood and collect food for my old, blind parents. At night, I make a fire and cook for them. That is all that I do," the man replied. Savitri said goodbye to Satyavan and returned to the palace to tell her parents that she had found the man she wanted to marry. Her parents were surprised that she wanted to marry a man of such simple means, but Savitri replied, "I do not care that he is not wealthy; he is a caring and loving man." Her parents agreed and soon plans were made for the two to be married.

Meanwhile, Satyavan worried that he had nothing to offer the princess. "Son, we never told you this, but your father was once the ruler of a kingdom of his own. His brother made us blind and stole the kingdom," said his parents. "You are rightfully a prince and love Savitri very much. You deserve to marry her."

Just before the wedding, the wisest sage in the kingdom announced to Savitri that Satyavan's stars were crossed and that he would die very soon. Savitri was devastated at the sage's news and begged him to tell her how she could change Satyavan's fate. The sage informed her that the only way she could save him was to eat only fruit, roots, and leaves; however, Satyavan would still die after one year.

Savitri and Satyavan were married and Savitri went to live a simple life with Satyavan and his parents. Every day, she ate fruit, roots, and leaves and nothing else. On the 1-year anniversary of their marriage, Savitri insisted that Satyavan take her with him to gather wood and find food. It was a hot day and Satyavan was hesitant to take Savitri, but Savitri persisted until Satyavan agreed. While Savitri and Satyavan were in the woods, Satyavan got a terrible headache. Savitri told him to rest under the shade of a banyan tree, but Satyavan soon died.

Savitri then saw Yamraj, the King of the Underworld, riding a water buffalo, coming for her husband's soul. Savitri told the banyan tree to look after her husband and followed Yamraj, who now had her husband's soul. Savitri begged Yamraj to take her soul as well, but he refused, so she continued to follow him.

"Stop following me and go away," said Yamraj. Savitri continued. "I can see that you are not going to give up easily. I will grant you one wish, but you cannot ask for your husband's soul," Yamraj stated. Savitri wished that her in-laws would have their sight back. Yamraj granted her wish and told Savitri to go home, but Savitri continued.

"You are really determined. I will grant you one more wish, but you are still not allowed to ask for your husband's soul back," reminded Yamraj. Savitri wished that her in-laws would have their kingdom back. Yamraj granted her wish and told Savitri to go home, but Savitri continued.

Yamraj was confused, as Savitri continued to follow him. "I will grant you only one more wish, but remember you cannot ask for your husband's soul." Savitri wished that she would be the mother of many sons. Yamraj agreed to her wish and told Savitri to go home, but Savitri continued.

"You have my only husband's soul, so I can never have many sons. You have granted me a wish that will never come true," stated Savitri. Exhausted and annoyed, Yamraj returned Satyavan's soul to his body.

Delighted, Savitri rushed to her husband underneath the banyan tree. "My headache is gone," said Satyavan. "Yes, thanks to the shade of the kind banyan tree. Let us return home. There is a surprise that awaits us," replied Savitri, and the couple returned home together.

Adjective Collections: Exploring Biases and Increasing Awareness of Asian American Parenting and Parent-Child Relationships

Type of Activity: 90-minute workshop

Educational Objectives
- Increasing awareness of assumptions and biases around parenting styles
- Learn about Asian and Asian-American parenting styles
- Consider how to apply learned material to work with Asian/Asian American clients

Adjective Collections will consist of three parts: (1) a small group discussion, (2) a large group adjective collection activity, and (3) large group discussion of the activity with excerpts from relevant literature and clinical recommendations. Through engagement in the experiential activity, participants will become aware of their own biases regarding parenting and parent-child relationships. Furthermore, participants will become aware of Asian American parenting and the relationships that Asian Americans have with their children. Clinical recommendations will include psychoeducation for immigrant families and their therapists; empathy and understanding surrounding the immigrant generation; responsibility taken by children and parents; acquiring skills via role playing and solution focused exercises; clients and therapists making informed decisions about the effects of acculturative family distancing (AFD); adapting psychotherapy to include culturally relevant information and interventions; and being aware of stereotypes.

Procedures

The workshop will begin with the larger group breaking into smaller groups. In these smaller groups, participants will be given the following questions for discussion: (1) what adjectives describe a good parent? (2) What adjectives describe a bad parent? (3) What are your experiences with good parents/parenting? (4) What are your experiences with bad parents/parenting? Each group will be asked to choose three adjectives that constitute a good parent and three that constitute a bad parent to share with the larger group. After the small groups have had time to discuss the topic of good parents and bad parents, the groups will come together into a larger group for the Adjective Collections.

Adjective Collections

During the Adjective Collections, the smaller groups will share with the larger group the three adjectives that describe a good parent and three adjectives that describe a bad parent. Workshop leaders will record these adjectives on a visible surface for the whole group to see, such as a white board. After all groups have given their adjectives, the workshop leaders will reveal a second list of adjectives. This list of adjectives will consist of Asian American parents' and children's description of what comprises good and bad parents. These adjectives will be taken from a literature review of articles and non-fiction texts on Asian American parenting and Asian American parent-child relationships. The authors suggest *Battle Hymn of the Tiger Mother* by Amy Chua (2011) as a key text.

Large Group Discussion

The large group discussion will focus on the participants' reactions to the adjectives/descriptors used by researchers of and authors. The workshop leaders will discuss the literature from which they selected their adjective list. The group will then discuss the activity and its meaning for them, both as a group and as individuals. Special attention will be paid to points where participants agreed and disagreed in their descriptors of good parents. Participants will be asked to discuss what they believe accounts for these differences and similarities. Participants will also be asked to think about their personal biases regarding parenting and talk within the group about how these biases may or may not be impacting their relationships with people from different cultures and/or ethnicities.

From Loss to Acceptance: Using Literary Memoir and Guided Imagery to Respond to Exclusion Experiences of Ethnic and Racial Minority LGB Clients

Type of Activity: 2-hour workshop

Educational Objectives
- Learn about the common experience of interpersonal loss for racial and ethnic minority LGB members
- Experience imaginal loss to help build empathy and understanding for others
- Consider how to apply understanding of potential relationship loss with clients

This experiential activity utilizes literary memoir and guided imagery to increase understanding of the common experience of interpersonal loss for ethnic and racial minority LGB members. Using a frame of their own valuable interpersonal needs, participants will reflect on the costs of familial rejection, social exclusion, and interpersonal redemption common in the lives of ethnic minority LGB individuals. The active discussion stimulated by the imagery exercise and the accompanying loss and redemption narratives will help participants to better understand potential relational stressors of ethnic minority LGB clients.

Procedures

The workshop begins with a brief reading of selected memoir excerpts from acclaimed ethnic and racial minority gay, lesbian, and bisexual authors. See the References list for the titles of some recommended books. Presenters then engage participants in a guided imagery experience in which participants reflect on key interpersonal relationships and meaningful experiences from their own lives.

Prompts to Aid in Identifying Key Relationships and Experiences

- What is the name of a person you rely on for comfort?
- What is your favorite place, and what feelings do you have when you are there?
- What is your happiest memory?
- What do you like most about yourself?
- What is your life dream?

Participants should then be guided by presenters to imagine the loss of these relationships, places, experiences, and qualities. Participants might prefer to journal during this time to process their own imaginal experiences of loss. Upon completion of the guided imagery activity, participants form small groups to reflect on the exercise. The small group conversations are facilitated by the presenters and will include adequate small-group debrief. The presenters should then remind the participants that these losses are imaginal. Participants are encouraged to tear up their personal list of "losses" while affirming to themselves that the relationships, memories, and dreams are still available to them.

Participants will reconvene in the large group and share the stories and themes they have created, followed by closing comments. Presenters will provide directions to guide the members of the small groups to communicate key points of their discussion with the larger group. This way the small groups will integrate though sharing experiences, ideas, conflicts, and resolutions and the group achieves wholeness, a common ground of acceptance, and redemption.

> **Discussion Questions on Loss**
> - What feelings or emotions surfaced during this activity?
> - How did it feel to tear up the different slips of paper?
> - Were there times when you struggled to tear up the paper or chose not to tear it up? Or did not want to tear it up but did. How did that feel?
> - In what ways, can you relate this exercise to your own life?
> - Can someone discuss a time when you held back information about who you are in fear that you may lose a friendship, job, or be ridiculed?
> - In what ways can we create communities were everyone feels safe and included?

Suggested Books of Fiction

Dole, M. L. (2008). *Down to the bone.* **Bella Books.**

Shai, a Cuban-American girl, is kicked her out of the house after getting caught texting her girlfriend. She is forced to fend for herself in Miami and is taken in by those who love and accept her. Shai must decide what is more important, pretending to be something she is not, or being faithful to her true self. Themes include self-identity and chosen families.

Lorde, A. (1982). Zami: A new spelling of my name—A biomythography. Crossing Press.

Depicts the powerful story of what it was like to be a young Black lesbian in the 1950s. Follows Audre from living with her parents (from the Caribbean island of Grenada), in Harlem, to working in a factory in CT, to living in Mexico to her return to NY. "Zami," is a Carriacou name for women who work together as friends and lovers. Themes include importance of relationships and how they all leave influence on one's life.

Satyal, R. (2009). *Blue boy.* **Kensington Publishing.**

Kiran Sharma is a 12-year old gay Indian American boy whose parents immigrated to Cincinnati from India. He finds an affinity with the Hindu god Krishna. He plans to have a triumphant unveiling of his "true" self as the modern-day embodiment of the Hindu god during an extravagant song and dance number at the annual elementary school talent show. Themes include feelings of separateness and confusion.

Schulman, S. (2008). *Rat Bohemia.* **Arsenal Pulp Press.**

Follows the stories of Rite Mae, a lesbian rat exterminator employed by the city, and David, a gay writer with AIDS. Their stories portray downtrodden and grieving gay and lesbian community in the wake of the AIDS epidemic in New York City. They tour their neighborhoods and are confronted by the devastating and numerous deaths of their chosen loved ones. Themes include familial judgment, abandonment, and cruelty.

Torres, J. (2011). *We the animals.* **Houghton Mifflin Harcourt**.

Details the struggles of a young adolescent as he comes to understand his sexuality amidst chaotic family circumstances, blue-collar over-worked young parents, and wild games with his brothers. At the end, the protagonist is placed in a psychiatric hospital for homosexuality by his parents. He reflects on the importance of his supportive teacher: "Laura saved me. She was always there for me, always the kind of light post. I have been in touch with her all through the years. You need somebody to remind you, Make this your priority." Themes include adolescent experience and pathologizing of homosexuality.

Scarf Dance

Type of Activity: 20-minute relaxation skill and "Ice Breaker"

Educational Objectives
- Learn mindful and movement-based relaxation activity

Independent activity in the beginning in an unfamiliar environment may result in feelings of isolation, fear, or awkwardness. This activity does not require independent, isolated actions, such as expressing their feelings or telling the story of trauma. This scarf activity within a group helps create a safe environment before approaching another activity. This scarf movement can be used as a warm-up exercise, in the beginning of all the activities and as closure at the end, to calm feelings and allow for a shift from the activity time to reality. It can be used by individuals who want to practice with movement-based relaxation.

Procedure

Create a calm and safe space for the group. Use comforting music and lighting, when possible. Provide participants with an assortment of scarf-like fabrics (the greater the assortment, the better). Allow participants to select a scarf and encourage them to use their senses to notice any soothing elements to the scarf they have selected.
- Create a circle (smaller circles may be created for a larger group) and tie the scarves end-to-end. Each participant will hold a piece of their scarf with both hand and slowly lift the arms while stepping forward towards the center of the circle. Step back as lower your arms. Notice the tension

and release of the muscles, and the rhythm of the breath with the movement. Repeat.

- Ask participants to hold their own scarves in their left hand and grab their neighbor's with their right hand. As they are linked together, have them walk counterclockwise, then clockwise. Next, they shall face the middle of the circle and walk inward and then back to their original position. These movements will go along with the music. Repeat.
- Untie the scarves and let each participant have their own. Open the scarf. Stay in the circle and make the same movement as you did with a group. Repeat.
- Make a ball with the scarf, toss above your head, and catch as it falls.
- Sit on the scarf in a circle. Wrap up your legs and arms like a ball. Open your body, spreading your arms and legs. Follow the music. Repeat.
- Stretch the scarves on the floor. Play music while participants move about the room (creative movement, like dancing or skipping encouraged). When the music stops, participants find another person's scarf to sit on. Repeat.
- Tie the scarf with other scarves on both sides. Roll the scarves from the person on the edge to make a big ball.
- If someone prefers to not play, they may watch the movement of others. It is encouraged that they keep their scarf so that they will be able to rejoin the activity easily if they wish.

Appendix B: Case Vignettes

Vignette 1: Champ

The following case is based on the semi-autobiographical novel by Jackson S. Mitchell (2013) The Residue Years. Bloomsbury.

Shawn, who goes by the nickname "Champ," is an African American man in his twenties who has agreed to participate in psychotherapy pursuant to his early release from a 16-month sentence for distribution of a controlled substance. While his overall prison term has been relativity uneventful, his mood was described as "inconsolable" following one of his mother's visits. Champ expressed several concerns about life after his release including housing, his relationship with his daughter, and a desire to finish his undergraduate degree. He is encouraged by his mother, who has maintained abstinent from drugs for many years and works a stable job.

Champ's mother, Grace, is approximately 40 years old and worked as an accountant during Champ's early childhood. She was married to Champ's stepfather Kenneth, and together they were able to provide Champ with a relatively happy childhood. However, Kenneth engaged in several incidents of infidelity and eventually Grace separated from him. While separated from his stepfather, Grace started abusing substances, and she and Champ moved often. He noted that every place they stayed in had at least one shut off notice for electricity, phone, or heat.

Champ was exposed to many incidents of Grace's substance abuse, which continued until the time of his arrest and involved several admittances to rehab facilities and prison. While Champ expressed deep love for his mother, her struggle with substance abuse has contributed to an overall ambivalent relationship. He noted, "…what happens when that first love warns you to save room for hurt and spends half your life applying the most harm?"

Champ noted that selling drugs did not start out to support himself. He explained that his mother got on drugs when he was ten years old. By the time he was thirteen or fourteen, he was exasperated by the things which were happening and thought, "If no one cares about my mother, then why should I care about theirs?" He said he felt victimized by drugs and that when he sold drugs, he felt like he had his own life in his hands.

Champ spent a considerable amount of time during the interview talking about identity. He also spoke about the necessity of having a nickname where he is from and how nicknames give one's life meaning. Champ indicated that his ambition to make a name for himself was common in his neighborhood. He was unable to make a name for himself in basketball, so he began to want to make a name for himself selling drugs. He stated, "I refuse to be one of these fools anonymous everywhere but inside their head." However, he described an environment that appeared to provide more opportunities for success through illegal mean than legitimate ones.

Before his arrest, Champ lived in an apartment with his pregnant girlfriend. They dated for about three years and during that time he described her as the best girlfriend he has had. Champ admitted to several incidents of cheating, and that he may have cheated on her because he did not deserve her and wanted her to leave. He currently does not talk to his ex-girlfriend and he has limited contact with his daughter.

Discussion Questions

- How does Champ have power and control of his life? In what ways might he not? What information are you using to inform these theories?
- In what ways might you address Champ's desire to make a name for himself as he considers letting go of one identity and starting to create a new one?

- What information about the U.S. Prison and Justice system might be helpful to consider in working with Champ?
- What barriers in attaining his stated goals might Champ face when released from prison?
- What are characteristics of Prison Culture? How might they be important?

Vignette 2: Sara

Sara is an 18-year-old transgender makeup artist and YouTuber who has come to therapy for stress due to her maternal grandmother's immigration to the United States from Japan. Sara's grandfather has just passed away and her grandmother is immigrating to New York City to live with Sara's family. Her grandmother does not know that Sara has transitioned from male to female and is also not aware that Sara has moved from New York City to Los Angeles for her career. Sara reports the guilt over her grandmother not knowing about her transition is causing debilitating stress. Sara reports that ever since she learned that her grandmother is immigrating to the United States, she has experienced "stomach aches, bad headaches, and a few panic attacks." Sara is an active member of the transgender community in Los Angeles, well known for her YouTube videos in which she discusses her transition. She has over half a million followers and she says they admire her for her makeup artistry skill set and for her zero-tolerance policy regarding cyber bullying.

Sara reported that she used to experience high anxiety and depressive episodes when she was younger. She said that starting around age 12 she would have intense and pervasive thoughts of wanting to die, especially when feeling overwhelmed or alone. Sara said that she did not reach out for support because she felt ashamed of her gender dysphoria and she feared she would be rejected by her family and community. Sara said that since she came out to her parents and started to present in a gender-congruent way, she has not had a full depressive episode.

Sara described worry that her grandmother might suffer from depression, especially since the passing of Sara's grandfather. Sara worries that her grandmother is under too many stressors, and Sara fears that her grandmother's health could be negatively affected when learning about Sara's transition, relocation, and career. Sara questions if it might be worth hiding her identity from her grandmother, as she has already kept it hidden from her for so long.

Sara noted that her panic is highest when she thinks of presenting herself as a male to her grandmother. She said that she has strong, visceral reactions to hearing her deadname, although she can often prepare herself to hear it when she calls her grandmother now. When asked, Sara said she has not discussed this with her parents, as she fears they will encourage her to hide parts of herself. Sara said that she has already been surprised with her parent's acceptance of her now, but she is acutely aware that they also do not seem proud of her (such as not using her name regularly in discussions, not sharing her popular videos on their social media, etc.). Sara deeply wants her parents to be proud of her; however, she feels she should be grateful for their acceptance. Sara describes worrying that she is asking too much of them, and that she should prioritize her family's health and wellbeing over her own.

Discussion Questions

- Based on the limited information in the vignette, for what diagnoses might Sara meet criteria at this time? What are the potential implications of these disorders?
- Do you notice any personal desire for Sara to manage her dilemmas in a specific way? If so, might your desire be informed by your own

> personal history and/or culture(s)?
>
> - What concerns might you have for Sara if she were to decide that presenting as male to her family is the best solution for her dilemma?
> - What factors are playing a role in Sara's strong desire to have her family feel proud of her? How might this differ if Sara came from a different background?

Vignette 3: Jackie

The following case is based on the novel by J. Woodson (2014), Brown Girl Dreaming. Penguin.

Jackie is an African American female in New York City. She reports feeling marginalized and discriminated by the White cultural community. Jackie's identity balances her strong worldly ambitions to establish a successful writing career, find a romantic relationship and form a family of her own. In addition, she feels pressured to conform to certain behaviors by her own family. She feels pressure from her mother to achieve successful integration with White society, and pressure from her grandmother to continue her religious practices and maintain her roots in the African American culture of the South. The modern urban African American culture creates an attractive allure that surrounds her budding artistic life in New York City. She describes feeling conflicted between the two sets of expectations.

Jackie is the second youngest of three children. Her family has moved several times during her childhood, and this has further exacerbated her cultural identity upheaval. After living her first few years of life in Ohio, her mother separated from her father and brought the children to her family's home in South Carolina. Jackie grew close with her grandfather who became the nurturing masculine presence that replaced her natural father.

In middle childhood, Jackie's mother traveled to New York City to start a new life and find better economic opportunities in a culture that was more racially tolerant. Jackie felt abandoned and resentful of her mother, especially when she found out her mother was pregnant, and Jackie would no longer be the baby of the family. While her mother was in New York, Jackie and her siblings were cared for by the stricter hand of her grandmother who soon enrolled them in religious activities of the local Kingdom Hall of Jehovah's Witness. Jackie gained a solid sense of discipline, faith and family values, and a strong moral code while working with the church. Though at times she felt that she was missing out on her childhood and she often yearns to be free of a nagging guilt anytime she is having fun, she still receives great sense of strength and belonging from her faith.

Jackie describes a mild depression that began during her adolescence. She experiences feelings of isolation and has a constant yearning for the love and connection she felt in her youth. Jackie first noticed feeling inferior when her baby brother was born, and she received less attention from her mother. She also experiences anxiety and low self-esteem when it comes to finding a career and interacting with less tolerant White people. This relates to the various incidents of prejudice she has experienced. More often than not, she felt like she and her family were treated as "outsiders" and ineligible for the same privileges of their White counterparts.

As strengths, Jackie has a strong family network. She feels that although they do not understand her, her mother, grandmother, and siblings would all be there to support her if she needed help. Though she struggled in more concrete subjects during school, like math and science, Jackie thrived with creative writing and other artistic subjects which became powerful outlets of expression and coping with difficulty in her life. She hopes that one day her writing can become a source of income for her, but she does not feel fully confident in her ability to become successful.

> **Discussion Questions**
>
> - What values are associated with Southern, rural communities? Northern, urban communities? How might these values fit the needs of the communities?
> - How might you apply the MCRC Model (Chapter 5) if you were to work with Jackie?
> - What special concerns might a White therapist need to address when working with Jackie?
> - How do the circumstances of her mother's relocation when Jackie was a child influence Jackie's internal conflict?

Vignette 4: Helen

The following case is based on L. See (2014) China dolls: A novel. Random House.

Helen is a 30-year-old Asian American woman who sought therapy due to difficulties within her interpersonal relationships. Helen struggles in developing and maintaining significant relationships and feels closed off from the world much of the time. As an Asian American woman, Helen has always struggled between remaining loyal to her traditional Chinese culture and upbringing, and the American culture she was born into. Caught between these two worlds, Helen often found herself doubting who she was and where she belonged.

When Helen was an adolescent, her family moved from San Francisco to their home of origin in China. At the age of 18, Helen married a young man through an arranged marriage. Soon after, Helen had her first child, named Dajun. Helen reported being very much in love with her husband and her child and worked hard to be a good wife and mother.

When the Japanese invaded China prior to the second World War, soldiers pillaged Helen's village. She watched as her husband and his family members were killed by soldiers and tried her best to get away and save her baby. Hiding in a rice paddy, a soldier found Helen and Dajun, and attacked with a bayonet. The wound was fatal for Dajun but Helen managed to survive. She was raped and beaten by enemy soldiers and left for dead. She managed to crawl her way to safety, but she reported that she was never able to recover from the guilt of being unable to protect her child.

Helen came home to her family in the United States, but she lived on as an embarrassment and a burden to her family. In her culture, a widow is looked after by her deceased husband's family and her son; without them, Helen had nowhere to go. Beyond this, she had no value as a woman who had been previously married. Returning to the United States provided Helen with a sense of safety and security; however, she had to live with the fact she was a disgrace to her family. Helen reports that she was continuously reminded that she was a "worthless daughter" by her father.

In her mid-twenties, Helen became unexpectedly pregnant after a brief relationship with an "Occidental" (White) man. Because of laws forbidding Occidentals to marry "Orientals" (Asians), Helen was left to deal with the pregnancy alone. Eddie, a friend and fellow nightclub dancer, offered to marry her so that she would be able to keep her child. Eddie was gay and this helped with his own ventures in the show business world. After they were married, they lived together at Helen's family compound where she had a second son, named Tommy.

Helen described a history of female friendships that had been influential in her life, but those relationships ended. Helen described that some of these issues might have been related to her own struggles. She described feeling chronically lonely and disconnected from people around her.

Discussion Questions

> - What historical and/or sociopolitical information about a war or conflict might you use to inform your work? When research is specifically lacking on wars/conflicts, in what ways might you generalize similar scenarios?
> - What factors do you consider to be potential barriers to Helen making and sustaining relationships? Do you consider these factors to be pathological?
> - How might you expect Helen's feelings of worthlessness to manifest in a therapy setting?
> - Given the law concerning marriage stated in the vignette, what other questions might you have about the systemic treatment of Asians in this period in the United States that might be influencing Helen's daily life?

Vignette 5: Chan-woo

Chan-woo is a Korean youth who had immigrated when he was five and became a ward of the state when he was 12 years old due to truancy, vandalism, and neglect. He lived with his brother and mother, who had suffered from domestic violence before leaving his father in Korea. His brother was physically abusive as he was the disciplinarian in absence of the father. Chan-woo's mother was often gone from the home due to working extended hours, although there was speculation from Chan-woo's treatment team that she might also suffer from mental health and substance abuse issues.

Chan-woo was taken into custody and was placed with a friend of the family until he was transferred to foster care due to continued acts of violence and vandalism. Chan-woo was aware that the family friend was asking that he be removed from the home, and that his mother had not complied with the state's mandates (such as her own personal counseling and a completion of a parenting course).

He was enrolled in an alternative school with case management supports, a counselor, and a social worker. Due to his extensive trauma history and acts of aggression, the team identified counseling as a resource, but Chan-woo did not initially want to engage.

The assigned social worker determined counseling to be an integral and required part of his treatment plan. After several counseling sessions, the case manager engaged him in a conversation about how he perceived therapy. The concept of talking about history and trauma was culturally a poor fit and the youth identified education, working-out, sports, and getting a job as more appropriate therapeutic activities. The social worker had a dilemma, as counseling had already been agreed on by the treatment team and discussed with the custodial magistrate.

Chan-woo began to act-out in sessions with the social worker. He first started to arrive to sessions late, and then he stopped coming entirely. His social worker tried to problem solve with his foster parent, such as having the adult watch him enter the building; however Chan-woo would often still not attend session. The social worker continued to work with the parent to get Chan-woo into session. However, Chan-woo refused to speak or would play music and videos on his phone at a high volume. His social worker felt lost on how to engage him and started to dread the appointments.

Chan-woo's foster parent then requested that his therapy be moved to a treatment center closer to their home. Chan-woo's social worker considered that a transfer to another provider could be helpful for them both. However, the treatment team was advocating for Chan-woo to continue with his current therapist for stability. At the next session, both Chan-woo and his social worker seemed unhappy with this decision.

Discussion Questions

- What might be underlying Chan-woo's social

worker's strong reaction?

- What are your experiences of strong personal reactions to clients? Do you believe these reactions could be attributable to cultural differences? How might you determine that something is a cultural difference versus and individual (personal) difference?
- How might the gender identity of the therapist influence the transference of Chan-woo?
- If you were the social worker, would you try to incorporate Chan-woo's identified therapeutic activities into a counseling session? If so, how?
- If you conducted Chan-woo's intake and had freedom to create an initial treatment plan, would you initially start with a treatment protocol for trauma or start with something more flexible? What factors would influence that decision?
- How would one go about seeing if a specific treatment protocol for trauma is appropriate for culturally diverse patients?

Vignette 6: Lila & Cua

Lila is a primary care psychologist meeting with Cua, a young Hmong woman referred for depression. Cua is a second-generation immigrant and has grown up in California. Lila begins the intake, and it is quickly apparent that Cua does not identify as depressed. She believes, as does her family, that she is suffering because one of her souls is missing. Lila initially wonders if she can be helpful to Cua, given that they are conceptualizing the problem differently.

Lila asks Cua to describe the problem in her own words and to explain how she would approach healing. Cua explains that various forms of sickness are the natural result when one of the many souls that reside in the body is lost. In her culture, a qualified religious person would bring her soul back.

Lila explores the patient's willingness to have a multi-pronged approach to healing. She wonders if Cua might consider 10 psychotherapy sessions as well as religious rituals with her family at their place of worship. Throughout the process Lila demonstrates curiosity and respect for Cua's beliefs and traditions. She overtly expresses empathy for Cua's challenges and helps her to develop a holistic plan that includes noninvasive Western treatment such as psychotherapy and sleep hygiene while also pursuing the curative practices common in her culture. Cua agrees to come back for another session and thanks Lila for supporting her in addressing her depression in a culturally relevant way.

Discussion Questions

- Are brief models of care appropriate for all cultural groups? How might you assess this if research is lacking?
- How might one quickly build a therapeutic alliance when there are vast cultural differences?
- What obligation, if any, does this therapist have in terms of coordinating this multi-pronged with religious leaders and Cua's family?
- In settings where notes are available to or automatically shared with patients, how would one talk about differences in opinion on etiology in a culturally sensitive way?

Vignette 7: Dr. Worthen & Tessa

Dr. Worthen, a university psychologist, met with Tessa, a twenty-three-year-old African woman from Sierra Leone presenting with symptoms of depression. Tessa travelled to the United States alone, leaving behind her parents, twin sister, and two younger brothers. She had arrived in the United States three months prior as an international exchange student. Tessa had no support system in the US and felt isolated and alone. Her depression was affecting her ability to perform academically and limiting her motivation to make friendships. She spent hours talking to family over the internet and was tearful after these conversations. By the time she came to the counseling center she was considering giving up on her education abroad and returning home.

After Dr. Worthen conducted an intake interview adhering to multicultural guidelines, Tessa and Dr. Worthen began a course of therapy paying particular attention to the challenges of acculturation. Tessa had been accustomed to witnessing abject poverty and, although, her family was considered middle class by Sierra Leonean standards, she had grown up with far less than even the poorest of her classmates. She struggled with the apparent waste she saw around the campus and found that she was often frustrated with her peers. In addition, Tessa did not expect to see her family except during the summer break because airfare was too expensive for her to return home more than once a year. Dr. Worthen, as a college counselor working at a university that prided itself on maintaining a diverse student body, felt competent working with students dealing with depressive symptoms because of both homesickness and feelings of cultural dislocation. However, Tessa's progress in therapy was slower than expected. Even after she began making friends and seemed to have a support system on campus, she would fall into bouts of depression that were getting worse with time.

Discussion Questions

- Based on the vignette, what Adverse Childhood Experiences might Tessa have experienced? How might you consider interpreting the scale when Tessa was "middle class" while in Sierra Leone,

> but "in poverty" by U.S. standards?
> - What factors do you think went into Dr. Worthen's timeline of expected progress in therapy? Which may have been overlooked?
> - Besides making friends and establishing a support system on campus, what are some other possible reasons for Tessa's worsening depression? What factors may be exacerbating her feelings of cultural dislocation?

Vignette 8: Bandile & Siphesihle

Bandile is a 10-year-old Black African boy living in South Africa post-apartheid. He was referred for psychological testing after his aunt, Siphesihle, expressed concerns. Specifically, he has been talking-back to his family, neglecting homework, and only washing certain parts of his body.

Bandile has been HIV+ since birth. He is aware of his HIV status; however, it is apparent that he may not understand the severity of the virus. Siphesihle reports that Bandile's mother passed away soon after Bandile was born. He is the youngest of three children. However, his brother and sister are grown and live out of the house. At that time, Siphesihle took Bandile in and began caring for him as her own son. Bandile lives in her home with Siphesihle, another aunt, and two uncles. Bandile's father lives in a shack outside of the house.

When describing Bandile as a young child, Siphesihle explained that he was "quiet," "not naughty," and always stayed close to his aunt. Bandile did not have any reported language development problems. There have been no neurological concerns noted; however, he has had many high fevers throughout his life.

Siphesihle said that Bandile "never" does his homework. Siphesihle described Bandile as avoiding his work until breakfast before school. At this time, he will begin to cry and Siphesihle often gives in and completes his homework. Siphesihle reported worrying that Bandile is unable to answer questions in class because he is not prepared.

Siphesihle reports that Bandile often makes careless mistakes and shows difficulty sustaining attention. He rarely listens when directly spoken to and does not complete any household chores. Bandile frequently avoids tasks requiring sustained mental effort and often loses his possessions. Siphesihle describes Bandile as being unable to sit still and is told by his teachers that he often leaves his classroom seat when it is not appropriate. He often runs around inappropriately and has difficulty engaging in leisure activities quietly.

Bandile has defaulted on ARVs many times, often for months at a time. Siphesihle reports that his father often takes from Bandile's ARV medication, even though he has not been officially diagnosed as having HIV. Bandile often tries to avoid taking his medication, and Siphesihle explained "shouting" at him when he does so.

Bandile is currently in the 5th grade. From first through fourth grade his marks were positive. However, during his 5th grade year, Bandile's marks have been getting progressively worse and his behaviour has been more of a concern. Currently, Siphesihle reports that Bandile is struggling with reading, spelling, arithmetic, written work, concentration, and attention, and study skills. With information from Bandile's teachers, Siphesihle reports that they like him, but explain that he is "naughty" in school.

Discussion Questions

- What top three considerations feel most important when assessing Bandile?
- How do you consider medical diagnoses in your work? What cultural identities might be helpful to

> consider when thinking about the psychological effects of physical health conditions?
> - What psychological diagnoses might you be thinking about with Bandile's behaviors at home and at school? Are there any confounding variables for those diagnoses?
> - How might sex roles be affecting Bandile's willingness to comply with instructions given by adults? How might this differ in other cultures?

Vignette 9: Ramos

Ramos was a 16-year-old, Latinx youth referred to therapy to address dysfunctional and violent behavioral problems. Ramos was initially referred to treatment by a local child protection services agency after Ramos attempted to stay at a homeless shelter without a guardian. At the time of referral, Ramos was on probation for violent assaults against others and had received court mandated residential treatment for his violent offenses. The child protection services agency referred Ramos to treatment to improve his decision-making skills and maintain his anger management treatment. Although Ramos did not feel he was currently making poor decisions, he agreed to treatment so he could speak to an unbiased person about personal issues and receive emotional support.

Since the age of 12, Ramos had been involved with the juvenile legal system for violent behavior. He had been charged with criminal threatening and violent assault numerous times and had caused injury to individuals that required hospital attention. After previously being removed from several programs, Ramos graduated from a residential treatment facility tailored to male youths with behavioral problems. Ramos reported he had not been violent nor gotten into trouble with the law in the six months he had been home from the program.

At the time of intake, Ramos was living with his

biological mother and stepfather. Ramos reported that he did not speak with his biological father, who Ramos described as addicted to heroin. Ramos' mother reported that Ramos' father was abusive towards her when Ramos was young, but that the relationship ended before Ramos entered school. Ramos described having a close relationship with his mother and a deep respect for all women. Ramos fought often with his stepfather and felt he was "controlling" and "unreasonable." Ramos said that had trouble connecting with his stepfather, who was entirely Spanish speaking, while Ramos described only moderate proficiency in Spanish. Ramos said that he often felt confused when his mother and stepfather argued, as he often could not understand all the details of their discussion.

Ramos reported that he was no longer concerned with his behavior and he felt that he was no longer violent. Despite this, Ramos often engaged in aggressive behavior such as verbally confronting individuals in a hostile manner, making threatening remarks, and sparring with his friends. Ramos reported that if he commits one more criminal offence, he will be sent to a juvenile detention facility. Although Ramos reported not wanting to be a violent person, he did not understand how his behaviors were inappropriate and could lead to violent behavior.

Discussion Questions

- How might the goals of a referring agency influence a clinical impression prior to meeting? Is that something you consider? How might Ramos's referral questions influence a clinical impression?
- What factors could contribute to Ramos's low insight into his identified inappropriate behaviors?
- What barriers might a therapist have in being able to feel empathy for and establish rapport with someone who presents like Ramos? How and

when should those barriers be overcome?
- How might a language barrier between two individuals within a family unit impact the larger family system?

Vignette 10: Sam & Jordan

Sam is a senior, Orthodox Jewish man who has been practicing psychotherapy for many years. Jordan is a senior, Baptist Black man referred to him for counseling. Jordan said that he had regularly consulted with his pastor for religious guidance throughout his life, but that he had not been able to attend church. Jordan had his driver's license forfeited for vision loss, and since then had not been able to attend services or attend pastoral counseling. Jordan described being very lonely and isolated since losing his transportation, and he and Sam decided together that the counselor would visit him in his home once a week for ten weeks.

The first time the counselor visited Jordan and Lily, his wife, he was unsure how his Jewish background would affect the counseling interactions. Sam was born in 1909, the fourth son of a lower-class Orthodox Jewish couple in Brooklyn, New York. Sam was active in his synagogue, including singing in the choir, and he had been a cantor for 35 years. Over the years, he had a strong referral network and found himself working largely with Jewish clients.

When Sam entered Jordan and Lily's apartment, he found few indications of their Baptist faith. They lived in a lovely but small, subsidized apartment near downtown in a New England city. It was full of books and was always extremely clean. To Sam's surprise, however, there were no crucifixes, religious art, prayer cards, and no other obvious signs that they were Christian. This confused Sam at first because Jordan had spoken about how much he missed church and his relationship with his pastor.

In session, Jordan spoke about how his early life

experiences shaped him. He and Lily were married in 1928. Lily became pregnant the following year, and Jordan worked two jobs to try to support them through the economic Depression. Lily miscarried the child, but they had little time to grieve together because of Jordan's work. Jordan said that he was grateful to have found work despite many Jim Crow laws, and he spoke about how there was more work when White men left for World War II. After a few minutes of talking to Jordan, Sam observed that he was a very smart man, and he also conjectured that Jordan must have felt quite distant from his wife because he was working so many hours.

Jordan spoke about how his faith got him through the darkest moments in his life. He described feeling profoundly depressed when Lily experienced the miscarriage, but that he had faith that God had a plan for them. He said that throughout his life he managed his despair with faith. He said that he had hoped his children or grandchildren would bring him to church when he gave up his license, and that he feels disappointed at how no one has helped. He said that he feels lonely and disconnected from both his community and, in some ways, to God.

In their work together, Sam was reminded of his own experience of living through World War II. Sam's faith had been shaken when he learned about the atrocities of the Holocaust. Sam had believed that God was both all-powerful as well as a God of goodness and love. Believing in these attributes of God, Sam questioned how God could allow millions of benevolent Jews to be murdered. Sam ultimately lost his faith in God, but he did not tell anyone. He, too, valued his religious community, and he speculated he would feel depressed if he ever lost it. He continued to sing as a cantor and never told his rabbi about the questioning of his faith.

Discussion Questions

- How might Sam's personal experiences be a strength when working with Jordan? In what ways might they pose potential pitfalls?
- How might transference and countertransference present between Jordan and Sam?
- Besides ease of access for the patient, in what ways could in-home counseling be more beneficial than counseling in an office? In what ways could it be less beneficial?
- How might Sam broach the subject of his personal expectations of Jordan's household? What doors might that open or close?

Note: We thank Sarajane Rodgers, Geisinger Medical Center, Department of Psychiatry, Danville, PA, for her contributions to Appendix B.

About the Authors

Gargi Roysircar, EdD, Professor Emerita, Antioch University, founded the Antioch Multicultural Center for Research and Practice in 2000. She provides counseling service and assessment in U.S. refugee and immigrant communities and international disaster settings. Her research focuses on disaster trauma and resilience, immigrant mental health, multicultural competencies, culturally informed practices, and disaster responders' self-care, which have resulted in more than 100 articles. Her instrument, the Multicultural Counseling Inventory (MCI), is the most frequently cited instrument among published multicultural competency scales. Dr. Roysircar was the first woman and Asian editor of the *Journal of Multicultural Counseling and Development* (2004–2011). She has received numerous awards, including APA's 2019 International Humanitarian Award, and she is a Fellow of five APA divisions.

Allyssa Lanza, Psy.D., currently works in private practice in Bethesda, Maryland. She graduated with her doctorate in clinical psychology from Antioch University New England. She previously worked at Veterans Affairs Medical Centers and has experience and interest in working with First Responders. She has practiced in Haiti and South Africa. She enjoys learning about international practices in psychology. Dr. Lanza is donating her portion of book proceeds to nonprofit organizations dedicated to serving people of color.